M D F
16
Hunter

THE HAWKER
Hunter

A COMPREHENSIVE GUIDE

by Paul Bradley

SAM PUBLICATIONS

The cover artwork, by John Fox, which has been specially commissioned for this Modellers Data File, shows a pair of Hunter F.5s, WP180 'F' and WP190 'E', of No 1 Squadron, returning from a sortie over their base at Nicosia, Cyprus, during the Suez Crisis, in November 1956, resplendent in the black and yellow 'Suez Stripes' applied to most RAF aircraft taking part in the operation. WP180 was damaged beyond economical repair by sabotage at Nicosia on 10 November 1956, and WP190 was later preserved at Stanbridge and repainted with the serial number WP180

MDF 16
The Hawker Hunter
by Paul Bradley

First produced in 2009 by SAM Limited, under licence from SAM Publications
Media House, 21 Kingsway, Bedford, MK42 9BJ, United Kingdom

ISBN 978-1-9551858-9-2

Typeset by SAM Publications, Media House, 21 Kingsway, Bedford, MK42 9BJ, United Kingdom
Designed by Simon Sugarhood
Printed and bound in the United Kingdom by Buxton Press, United Kingdom

The MDF Series

- No.1 – De Havilland Mosquito *
- No.2 – Hawker Hurricane *
- No.3 – Supermarine Spitfire (Part 1: Merlin-Powered) *
- No.4 – Avro Lancaster (Inc Manchester & Lincoln)
- No.5 – Supermarine Spitfire (Part 2: Griffon-Powered)
- No.6 – Bristol Beaufighter
- No.7 – English Electric Lightning
- No.8 – Gloster (& Armstrong-Whitworth) Meteor
* Out of print

- No.9 – Messerschmitt Bf 109 (Part 1 Prototype to E Variants)
- No.10 – Messerschmitt Bf 109 (Part 2 F to K Variants)
- No.11 – British Aerospace Sea Harrier
- No.12 – The F-4 Phantom II (Part 1: USAF)
- No.13 – The F-4 Phantom II (Part 2: US Navy & Marine Corps)
- No.14 – The F-4 Phantom II (Part 3: Overseas Operators)
- No.15 – The Grumman F-14 Tomcat

Acknowledgments

Books of this nature are rarely the product of one hand and so it is with this one. I have received great support from many people in the production of this volume, but special mention needs to be made now to Srecko Bradic and Mark Gauntlett, without whom this book would have been much the poorer. Thank you both, my friends!

Much assistance was proffered to this rookie author by the good folks at SAM Publications and many thanks in particular to Neil Robinson and Gary Hatcher for their support, and to Simon Sugarhood for turning my raw material into this readable form.

Many enthusiasts offered help and photos. Special mention must be made to Greg Wilson and John Davidson for literally going out of their way in getting detail photos, while John Adams was a big help with his photos and technical knowledge.

The following rendered valuable assistance in one form or another – thank you all: James Perrin, Jim Bates, Matt Bacon, Edgar Brooks, Nikko Yaginuma, Nick Filippone, Chris Hall, Dave Wadman, Philippe Jacques, Steve Legassik of Northern Lights, Mat Potulski of Hawker Hunter Aviation, Dawn Cubin of Delta Jets, Nico Braas, Dave Smith, David Griffin and Chris Payne. Thanks also to Robert Hodgson, Jack Cook, Mick Gladwin and all at the Burek, LetLetLet, WIX, UAMF and Britmodeller forums for their help. To anyone who I have may have forgotten here, my apologies and thanks. And grateful thanks to the various personnel and offices of the following air forces for the use of materials: Switzerland, Lebanon, Chile, and Singapore.

Finally, but by no means least, a big thank you and hugs to my wonderful family – my wife, Danielle, and daughter, Robin, for putting up with my hobby!

Paul Bradley
February 2009

SAM PUBLICATIONS

Contents

Introduction

The Hawker Hunter – an evocative name for generations of pilots, aviation enthusiasts and modellers; a name that conjures visions of black arrows and blue diamonds; blue notes and smooth silhouettes. Her curvaceous lines at once a perfection of form and function.

Yet this most beautiful product of aeronautical engineering very nearly failed. Like many of her contemporaries, her early life was a struggle against the limits of knowledge. Through sheer will and persistence, the obstacles were overcome and this most successful of British jet fighters was able to flourish.

Now, some sixty years after her conception, this remarkable aircraft is finding new roles and useful life around the globe. The Hawker Hunter – truly the best of British.

Paul Bradley
February, 2009

An RAF FGA.9 stages through Malta. It's clean condition and lack of identifying markings makes it likely that this is a brand-new airframe on its way to serve with one of the Middle East Air Force squadrons *(© WA Harrison Collection)*

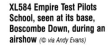

XL584 Empire Test Pilots School, seen at its base, Boscombe Down, during an airshow *(© via Andy Evans)*

Hunter T.8, XE664 '708' of No 764 NAS, Fleet Air Arm, based at Lossiemouth circa 1959. XE664 was converted from an ex-RAF single-seat F.4 (© John Fox)

Development of the Hunter

Chapter 1

Pre-Hunter History

The Hunter story properly begins back in 1944, when Hawker's Chief Designer, (Sir) Sidney Camm started work on a jet-powered version of his Fury fighter. Initially, the idea was to directly replace the Bristol Centaurus piston engine in the nose with a Rolls-Royce B.41 (later Nene) centrifugal jet engine exhausting from the underside of the cockpit, rather in the style of the Soviet Yak-15. This crystallized into the P.1035, where the Centaurus was replaced by a mid-fuselage mounted Nene with intakes on the side of the fuselage and a straight-through jet pipe exhausting under the Fury tail unit. The cockpit was moved forward on the nose and the forward fuselage bore more than a passing resemblance to the later Sea Hawk. Like the Fury, the aircraft would have had a tail-dragger undercarriage and in many respects would have been Hawker's equivalent to Supermarine's Attacker.

The P.1035 would have been a very limited machine and in an effort to produce a worthwhile aircraft, Camm evolved the design to include a bifurcated jet pipe. Split to exit on either side of the fuselage just aft of the wings' trailing edges, this offered a number of advantages, most notably a decrease in the loss of power often experienced with longer jet pipes, and the ability to add a small fuel tank in the rear fuselage, which was worthwhile considering the thirsty nature of early jet engines. Ironically, the return to the straight-through jet pipe on the Hunter contributed to a chronic lack of fuel capacity in the early versions!

Having switched to a split jet pipe, the horizontal tail needed to be raised to prevent the exhaust from interfering with the smooth operation of the elevators; this was raised to a mid-fin position. As the jet pipes increased the thickness of the wing trailing edge roots, this depth was extended forward, and the intakes were made part of the wing leading edge root rather than extensions of the fuselage sides. The complex elliptical wing inherited from the Fury was abandoned for a simple

tapering design with straight leading and trailing edges. The other major airframe change was a switch to a tricycle undercarriage to improve take-off and landing characteristics.

This redesign resulted in a new designation, the P.1040. Offered to the Air Ministry in October 1945, the design was rejected as being an insufficient advance on the existing Meteor and Vampire aircraft then in service with Fighter Command. Undeterred, Camm navalized the prototype by fitting folding wings and arrestor hook; accepted by the Royal Navy for the Fleet Air Arm under Specification N.7/46, and first flown in September 1947, this became the Sea Hawk.

The Sea Hawk was a very successful aircraft. Virtually vice-free and well-liked by its pilots, the Sea Hawk was produced in large quantities and was exported to Germany, the Netherlands and India, where it saw combat in the 1965 and 1971 Wars with Pakistan. Nevertheless, the Sea Hawk was still what is now termed a 'first-generation' jet aircraft, and suffered from a lack of range and store-carrying ability, to the point where the aircraft could carry drop tanks or bombs, but not both, when operating in the tropics or when there was a lack of wind speed over the carrier deck. The aircraft was also no match for the latest Russian fighters such at the MiG-15; this was a big concern prior to the Sea Hawk's very active participation in the Suez Campaign of 1956, as the Egyptians had recently received large numbers of the Soviet fighter. Sea Hawk pilots practiced pre-dawn take-offs in order to arrive over their targets before the MiGs' daily 'dawn patrols.' Luckily, no MiGs were ever encountered and no Sea Hawks were lost in aerial combat.

The Sea Hawk's obsolescence had been foreseen, and by using captured German aerodynamic knowledge, a swept-wing version of the P.1040 was planned. Designated as the P.1052, this was in essence a Sea Hawk fuselage and tail married to a new 35-degree swept wing. Two prototypes were ordered and the first of these, VX272, first took to the air in November 1948. Trials of this were very successful, with the aircraft reaching 650 mph in level flight, and were extended to full carrier operational trials on board HMS Eagle in 1952; there

The Hawker Sea Hawk can be regarded as an ancestor of the Hunter. Here, the Fleet Air Arm Historic Flight's WV908 waits for her display spot

Hunter F.1 WW604/F of
2330CU outside the workshop
sheds and F-Type hangars at
Pembrey in 1956 (© Ted Gauntlett)

was even talk of a production version, but rapid developments overtook the P.1052 and the aircraft was retired after a landing accident in 1953. This aircraft survives in storage at the Fleet Air Arm Museum in Yeovilton.

The continuing rapid advance in aerodynamic research saw the second P.1052, VX279, redesigned with swept tail surfaces; it also featured a straight-through jet pipe for its intended engine, the afterburning Tay, although delays in that engine's development led to VX279 retaining a less powerful Nene 2 during its life. Adopting the designation of P.1081 and flying in June 1950, this was a great advance on the Sea Hawk with a top speed in excess of Mach 0.89 at 36,000 ft. In fact, the P.1081 was seriously considered for production, drawing interest from the Australian Government which was looking for an advanced fighter to replace the badly outclassed Meteor F.8 then in service with the Royal Australian Air Force (RAAF) in Korea. However, dithering and prevarication in British governmental circles, of the sort that plagued British postwar technological developments in many fields, and continued problems with the Tay condemned the program after VX279 suffered a fatal accident in April 1951, claiming the life of Hawker's Chief Test Pilot 'Wimpy' Wade. His place was taken by Sqn Ldr Neville Duke. Notwithstanding the loss of the aircraft, flight data from the P.1081 program was usefully applied to another Hawker project, the P.1067. It was this project that would evolve into the Hunter.

Design of the P.1067 began as early as 1946, when Hawker drew up a new design to Specification F.43/46. This was originally for a twin-engined aircraft – early jet engines developed poor thrust – but Hawkers designed their proposal around the new Rolls-Royce AJ.65 axial-flow engine – later known as the Avon. This promised to deliver as much thrust in a single unit as a pair of the Meteor's Derwent engines, and using just one engine reduced airframe size, weight and drag. The original proposal was for a nose intake, all-swept flying surfaces including a T-tail, and an armament of four 20mm Hispano cannon. Maximum speed was projected at Mach 0.88. This was presented to the Air Ministry in early 1948. The Ministry was so impressed by the P.1067 that they rewrote the Specification around it, redesignating it as F.3/48. This called for a single-seat bomber interceptor armed with two 30mm ADEN or four 20mm Hispano cannon, capable of Mach 0.94

with an endurance of at least 75 minutes, sufficient for a climb to 45,000ft and 10 minutes combat. Power was to be from either the Rolls-Royce AJ.65 (later the Avon) or the Metrovick/Armstrong-Siddeley Sapphire. Other equipment was to include an ejection seat and ranging radar.

Prototypes

Development continued apace, and the Ministry ordered three P.1067 prototypes in June of 1948. At this time, the P.1067 looked nothing like the Hunter we know today, but a steady series of aerodynamic improvements was made. As 1949 progressed, the nose intake had been replaced by a bifurcated intake much like the Seahawk's and the tailplane had been moved to a position halfway down the fin. As work on the Avon had run into difficulties, the Sapphire engine was worked into the programme as an alternate powerplant. Two of the prototypes would use the Avon while the third was based around the Sapphire. The rear fuselage was removable to aid with engine maintenance and changes. Added punch was given by switching to 30mm Aden cannon, housed in a removable pack under the nose. No thought at this time was given to integrating air-to-air missiles into the design, missile technology at this time being in its infancy.

The P.1067 was to be constructed in five major assemblies: the front fuselage including the cockpit; centre fuselage including fuel tanks; rear fuselage with tail assembly; and the

A model of the P.1081 VX279,
made by Chris Payne
(© Chris Payne)

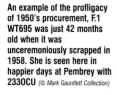
port and starboard wings. The aircraft would also have the now-standard tricycle undercarriage with single wheels on each leg, the nosewheel to retract forwards and the main gear retracting inwards into bays set into the wings. The canopy featured good vision with framing only on the forward edge and undersides; the rear of the canopy was unframed, but had an inflatable seal to retain pressurization.

Actual construction of the first prototype, WB188, was started in 1950 at the main Hawker plant at Kingston in Surrey, from where it was transported by road in June of 1951 to the Aeroplane and Armament Experimental Establishment (A&AEE) at Boscombe Down in Wiltshire for ground trials and initial flights; Hawker's old airfield at Langley, Bucks, was too small and the company's new test field at Dunsfold in Surrey was incomplete at this time. Assembly took some time and a couple of minor problems were worked on, delaying flight trials for a few weeks. Finally, painted in a very pale green (Similar to Sky) unique to the first two Hunters, WB188's maiden flight took place on July 20th, 1951, in the hands of Sqn Ldr Neville Duke.

The flight lasted 47 minutes; Duke took the aircraft to Mach 0.88 and 32,000 feet and performed some basic manoeuvres. His reaction to the new type was very positive, stating that it handled beautifully. His only concerns were some vibration emanating from the rear of the aircraft at high subsonic speeds, and the slick airframe's inability to

decelerate quickly – there being no provision in the design for a proper airbrake.

Aside from these issues, early testing was remarkably trouble-free and Duke showed off WB188 to the world at the 1951 Farnborough Air Show less than two months after its first flight. In April of 1952, Duke took the Hunter through the sound barrier in a shallow dive on a flight over Southern England.

The second prototype, WB195, made its maiden flight on May 5th, 1952. This aircraft was more representative of the production Hunter F.1, having a gun pack and radar gunsight fitted, as well as a production Avon 107 engine. WB195 was also used to trial various airbrake options. The third of the trio of prototypes, painted in High Speed Silver, was the Sapphire 101-powered WB202, which took to the air on November 30th the same year. This aircraft was also outfitted to production standards as an F.2, and was used for the initial Hunter gun-firing trials – an unfortunate choice as it turned out!

Mk 1 and 2
Even before WB188 was ready to fly, the Air Ministry issued a production contract to Hawker for an initial 198 airframes, later increased to 400. With the outbreak of the Korean War in June 1950, the British Government woke from its post-WWII slumber and realized the shortcomings in British military strength. In order to get the best equipment into service as quickly as possible, it set up a Super Priority production

scheme, with the Hunter and Supermarine's Swift as the backbone of its commitment to fighter strength. With 400 aircraft on order, production was split between three factories. The first production aircraft, F.1 WT555, left the Kingston works in May of 1953, followed in October by the first of 45 F.2s, WN888, from Armstrong Whitworth's Bitteswell works. The third production line, at Hawker's second factory at Squire's Gate, Blackpool, also produced the F.1 and their first aircraft, WW599, emerged in May of 1954. A fourth production line at Glosters was cancelled, as the company was unable to find the capacity to produce them due to other pressing commitments. 113 F.1s were built at Kingston and 26 at Blackpool, for a total of 139. The remaining airframes from the initial production orders were completed as Mk 4 and 5 aircraft.

With Hunters pouring off the production lines, the type was evaluated by various service institutions and it was at this point that two serious problems emerged. The first manifested itself very early in service trials. The Hunter was designed to use its flaps as airbrakes, but in practice it was found that

side-mounted intakes, causing hot, turbulent air to disturb the normal flow of air into the compressor, causing localized blade stall. Curing this would have entailed a major redesign of the intake region, which was not considered desirable, so Rolls-Royce were asked to come up with a solution involving the engine. A temporary resolution was to restrict fuel flow when the guns were fired, slowing the engine and leading to a significant loss of thrust. Pilots were restricted to speeds of less than 250 knots and heights under 25,000 feet when conducting weapons firing, rendering the F.1 useless in its intended role. Not until the F.4 introduced the more surge-resistant Avon 115 was the problem contained, but the problems of engine surging were not fully cured until an automatic fuel system and a flexible throttle control system were introduced with the F.6.

Another problem associated with cannon-firing was the tendency for the muzzle blast to cause the nose to pitch down. The solution for this was found after a series of trials; each cannon muzzle was fitted with a deflector box that pushed the muzzle blast down from the nose and away from the aircraft.

deploying these produced serious, and to the pilot very alarming pitch-down – not something you wanted to happen in the landing circuit and a liability in combat manoeuvering. In an attempt to counteract this, WB188 was fitted with various experimental air brakes, including a pair fitted on each side of the rear fuselage. The ideal position was found to be on the underside of the rear fuselage and the now-familiar ventral airbrake was fitted to the 19th production aircraft and all subsequent Hunters. While this was aerodynamically the best position for the air brake, it did mean that the brake could not be used when the aircraft was landing for fear of it being damaged by ground contact and an electrically-operated disabling system was used to retract the brake when the undercarriage was extended. While the airbrake was thus retracted when the Hunter was on the ground, loss of pressure in the hydraulic system meant that the brake could often be seen partially open on the ground, until the system was repressurized on start-up.

The second was a serious blow to the abilities of the Hunter as a weapon of war – firing the guns at altitude would cause the Avon fitted to the F.1 to surge badly, and even flame out. With the cannon fitted under the nose, gases were drawn into the

Yet another issue with the armament system was caused by the discarded ammunition belt links and shell cases. When being ejected from the aircraft, both the links and cases would strike the rear under-fuselage, causing damage. The solutions were quite simple compared to the other problems associated with the Hunter. The links, rather than being discarded, were collected in large pods under the nose. Their bulging appearance caused them to be given the nickname 'Sabrinas' after a well-endowed B-list actress of the period. These were retrofitted to the Mks 1 and 2, and fitted as standard from the F.4 onward. To solve the problem of errant shell cases, Hawkers simply lengthened the ejection tubes by a few inches, causing the shells to be ejected further into the aircraft's wake.

Perhaps the worst problem of all was the Hunter's dire lack of fuel. Despite the Air Ministry's specification asking for an endurance of 75 minutes, in reality, this was far too little to make the Hunter an effective combat aircraft, and Hawkers miscalculated the amount of fuel that the Avon would burn, leaving the F.1 with just about an hour's worth of fuel. A number of early Hunters were lost through running out of fuel, the worst instance occurring in February 1956, when a flight of Hunters was forced to divert from their destination by bad

weather; 6 aircraft crashed, four pilots ejecting and one being killed. While the fuel capacity of the F.1 and 2 was not altered, trials with 100-gallon drop tanks were initiated with WB202 in January 1954, and these were fitted from the F.4 and 5; meanwhile additional internal tanks were added in later marks, so that the late-mark FGA.9 had a very respectable ferry range, and an adequate combat radius.

While this litany of serious problems might seem to be a damning indictment of Hawker's design staff, the fact of the matter is that the fifties were a time of great change in aircraft design. No aircraft is perfect, and most designs worldwide had flaws that needed ironing out before the aircraft was deemed ready for service. Some never made it at all, while others became highly successful. Pilots generally liked the Hunter, remarking on its generally excellent performance and handling, while the airframe was simple and rugged for easy maintenance.

The issues outlined above highlight the rush to get the Hunter into service and the lack of prototypes which hindered thorough pre-service testing. With the Hunter ordered off the drawing board, the first 20 production aircraft had serious flaws but were useful in aiding various service establishments in revealing problems that could be translated into production line fixes. While not an ideal solution, this did point the way to the large pre-production batches of aircraft of more recent vintage. The fact that the Hunter went on to become one of the most successful fighters of the 1950s highlights the basic soundness of the design.

Mk 3

The sole Hunter F.3 was in fact the modified first prototype, WB188 and introduced an afterburning Avon RA.7R engine. WB188 was taken in hand in 1952 and fitted with new wing fuel tanks, lateral air brakes in the continuing quest to find the ideal position for these, and the new engine. This was in support of a projected supersonic variant of the Hunter, the P.1083. Projected performance figures were so good that Hawkers were encouraged to make an attempt on the World Air Speed Record, which at the time was held by a North American F-86A Sabre and stood at 670.8 mph. During WB188's conversion, this target was raised to 715.75mph by an F-86D.

The aircraft was ready by August 1953, and was flown to Tangmere in Sussex where final preparations were made and trial runs were made over the mandated 3 kilometre course off the south coast between Bognor Regis and Worthing. Special measures were taken to further improve the aerodynamics of the aircraft. A sharply pointed nose cone was fitted, as was a more sharply-swept windscreen – though this was not used on the record run – and the air brakes were skinned over. The cannon pack was removed, reducing weight. WB188 was also painted with a highly-polished coat of gloss red paint. On September 7th, the aircraft was pronounced ready, and as weather conditions were ideal, an attempt was made. Duke took the bright red Hunter to an average speed of 727.63 mph, or Mach 0.92. The timing was perfect – it was Press Day at the Farnborough Air Show!

This record lasted only until September 28th, as

Delta Jets' T.7 WV318 cavorts over the Gloucestershire sky. She flew in these colours at the 1960 Farnborough airshow as a member of 111 Squadron's Black Arrows
(© courtesy Delta Jets)

Supermarine had also been eying the record with their Swift. Lt Cdr Mike Lithgow went to the higher temperatures of Libya to push his modified Swift F.4 to 735.5mph. Some consolation for Hawkers and Duke was a new 100 km closed course record of 709.2mph, set on September 19th. After this record, WB188 was retired, to eventually end up, most fittingly, at the Tangmere Aviation Museum where she is displayed at the time of writing.

While finding fame as a record breaker, the Mk 3's development was otherwise wasted – the government of the day cancelled the supersonic Hunter program.

Mk 4 and 5

With the F.1 and 2 being rushed into service, many problems were discovered as outlined above. Some of these fixes were incorporated into the production lines, and resulted in the aircraft being redesignated as the F.4 and 5, the F.4 having an Avon engine, while the F.5 had a Sapphire. The F.4 and 5 were intended as minimum-change modifications in order to avoid disrupting the production lines. The most important changes were to fuel capacity and engine modifications. .

In the F.1 and 2, the wings were dry, but in order to increase range, eight small tanks were incorporated into the wing structure, giving an increase in capacity from 337 to 414 gallons. Each wing was also locally strengthened and plumbed to carry a pylon for an external 100-gallon fuel tank just outboard of the undercarriage. Trials were conducted for carrying bombs and unguided rockets, but these were not used by RAF service aircraft.

To alleviate the engine surging problems, Rolls-Royce had produced an improved Avon, the Mk 115, with surge-resistant features. These weren't available right away, and many F.4s were fitted with the earlier Mk 113 on the production line, then retro-fitted when the 115 became available. The last production F.4s had the much-improved Avon Mk 121. Deliveries of the Mk 4 started in March of 1955; a total of 349 Mk 4s were built, 173 at Kingston and 176 at Blackpool. The first F.4 squadron was 98 Sqn in March of 1955, while the initial F.5 user was 263 Sqn, in the same month. At the height

of their service, 20 RAF squadrons were equipped with the Mk 4, the majority going to RAF Germany.

The F.4 and 5 also introduced an follow-up tailplane to refine pitch control; this had been trialled on the F.1 but not introduced until later to avoid disruption to the production lines.

In August 1956, Sqn Ldr Roger Topp took his F.4 WT739, to a new Edinburgh-to-London speed record, at an average of over 717mph. This record stood until 1987, when it was finally broken by two F-4 Phantoms.

The F.5 was to the F.2 as the F.4 was to the F.1. While the Sapphire did not suffer the same surging problems as the Avon, the F.2 was also short on endurance so the F.5 was fitted with the new wet wing. As the Sapphire was a perfectly adequate engine, the F.5 retained the F.2's Sapphire 101. While the F.5 had the best performance and range of any Hunter to date, only 105 were built starting in 1955; these equipped 5 RAF squadrons. For some reason, it doesn't appear to have occurred to anyone to retro-fit the new wings to the F.2 and in effect create more F.5s; as a result, F.2s were unceremoniously scrapped, often with very low flying hours – a shame considering the acute shortage of airframes for conversion that was later suffered.

Mk 6

While the F.4 was much improved over the F.1, there was still room for improvement, particularly with the Avon that still had surging issues. Continued development by Rolls-Royce led to the new Series 200 Avon, with a new compressor section that owed much to the Sapphire; an automatic fuel delivery system; and an improved throttle management system finally cured the Hunter's surging problems for good. The Avon 203 also had much improved thrust, producing some 10,000lbs compared to 7,500 for the Avon 104 and 8,000lbs for the Sapphire 101.

As the Series 200 Avon had a larger diameter jet pipe, the tail cone was revised, and some fuel tanks were moved around. At the same time, fuel tankage was again increased, giving a total internal capacity of 390 gallons, giving a considerable increase in range and endurance. Another new feature with the Avon 200 was the introduction of an AVPIN (AViation Plessey

T.8 XL584/877 1984 – the tail of the GA.11 behind shows the old EDSG/White scheme, and is awaiting its next major service to be repainted in the overall Dark Sea Grey colours exhibited by 877. Tragically, 877 was lost just a couple of months after this photo was taken, with of her pilot
(© via Andy Evans)

T.8 WT799 based at Brawdy with an unidentified Fleet Air Arm squadron. This airframe can still be seen – by divers! She currently resides at the bottom of a lake near Doncaster for use by Scuba divers *(© WA Harrison Collection)*

Isopropyl Nitrate) engine starter system in place of the previous cartridge starter.

The first F.6, XF833, was flown in January 1954, before the F.1 was even cleared for service. However, the new Avon was plagued by a series of failures, which while eventually cured, did delay the production of the new mark. Six F.1 airframes were modified as pre-production F.6s, the first of these being flown in March 1955, while the first true production F.6, XE526, was flown in October 1955.

Initially, Mk 6 aircraft were fitted with standard F.4 wings, but a new wing was introduced on the production line, and retro-fitted to earlier machines. Dubbed the Mod. 228 wing, this featured additional wet-mount pylons outboard of the existing pylons. The inner pylons were strengthened to carry a new 230-gallon tank, but these interfered with flap operation and were only used for ferrying; normally, 100-gallon tanks would be used on each pylon. In any case, range was considerable extended so that a Hunter could now in theory fly non-stop to bases in Libya or Cyprus, a distance of over 1,500 miles.

A further modification to the wings was the now-distinctive outboard leading edge extension, or 'dog-tooth,' that cured a tendency for the Hunter to pitch up in turns. Late-production F.6 were also fitted with an follow-up tailplane that aided control in the transonic flight regime, though the elevators were retained.

Over 380 were built, but this number was much lower than planned, as the 1957 defence cuts led to the cancellation of 150 machines. At its height, the F.6 served with 18 frontline RAF squadrons, being replaced in the interceptor role by the Lightning.

Mention must be made of a late development of the F.6 for the RAF's Tactical Weapons Unit (TWU), which used the Hunter for weapons training from RAF Brawdy in south Wales. Due to generally poor weather and a lack of suitable diversionary airfields in the area, it was obvious that the unit's F.6s needed more endurance, and would need to carry the large 230-gallon tanks used by the FGA.9. In enabling these tanks to be fitted, the aircraft also needed to have the brake parachute fitted, and the flaps needed to have the inboard section cut away. In effect, the F.6s were converted to FGA.9 standard; 24 F.6s were taken in hand by Hawkers for these modifications. Interestingly, these aircraft were not relabelled as FGA.9s but flew with an F.6A designation.

Mk 7, 8 and 12

During the 1950s most front-line RAF types did not have a two-seat trainer version; it was thought that the existing two-seat Vampire and Meteor trainers were adequate for the task of converting fighter pilots to jets. Early Hunter pilots came from Meteor T.7s or Vampire T.11s and were given a quick tour of the Hunter cockpit by an old hand on their squadron then told to take her for a spin. However, advances in fighter technologies were rapidly outpacing the abilities of these venerable types, and so the RAF began to look at the possibility of a more advanced trainer for operational conversion units (OCUs) and turned to Hawkers. By coincidence, Hawkers had already initiated a two-seat Hunter project, the P.1011, for the export market, using their own money. The RAF issued a requirement in 1954 based on the P.1011, designated T.157D.

The P.1011 evolved through a series of configurations, but Hawkers and the RAF settled on a side-by-side seating arrangement; this gave the instructor a clear view of the student's actions and aided communications. An initial mock-up was assembled in 1955, initially with a double-bubble canopy, but this proved aerodynamically unstable and much testing was needed to come up with the single-piece production canopy. Even then, there were issues with buffeting that were cured by adding a deep spine aft of the canopy, smoothing the airflow towards the tail. The whole process went through over 20 different configurations and took over a year to solve, greatly delaying service entry.

The rest of the fuselage was based on the F.4, with an Avon 121 or 122 engine, but with a brake parachute housing above the tailcone. Production aircraft featured a single cannon on the starboard side. Although the prototype, XJ615, had standard F.4 wings with the straight leading edge, all 45 new-build T.7s were built with the Mod 228 wing with dog-tooth

the second prototype P.1011, G-APUX, was based on a former-Belgian F.6 airframe, the Hunter's modular construction aiding the conversion as all that was required were the new nose and tailcone. This particular airframe was used as a demonstrator and was loaned to many air forces prior to their adoption of the type – she served with at least 6 air forces around the world before being converted to a Chilean T.72.

India was the first customer for the improved trainer, specifying two cannon in place of the single gun of the RAF machines. Most export trainers were built to this standard and were converted from redundant F.4 and F.6 airframes. In addition to the 65 new-build trainers for the RAF and RN, Hawkers built 10 for the Netherlands, two for Denmark, one for Jordan, and 22 for India; all other two-seaters were conversions.

Finally, mention must be made of a singular two-seater, the T.12. This was converted from an FGA.9, having an Avon 203, and serialled XE531. Intended to support the TSR.2, it was given a more modern cockpit and avionics, and could be

and four pylons. Deliveries started to 229 OCU in May 1958, and most front-line Fighter Command Hunter squadrons also received a single T.7 for conversion and continuation training.

The Royal Navy watched development with interest, as it was introducing new high-performance fighters into service at the same time and required something with a bit more zip than the Sea Fury and Vampire trainers then in service. Ten aircraft were diverted from the initial RAF order and designated as the T.8. These were basically the same as the T.7, but had a different electronics fit and were equipped with an airfield arrestor hook under the tailcone. The T.8 was not intended to land on aircraft carriers - the undercarriage was not strengthened to allow this – but could be used to simulate carrier landings on fields equipped with an arrestor wire. These ten aircraft were followed by later conversions of F.4 airframes, a total of 30 more in various sub-types. The T.8B had TACAN navigation equipment, while the cannon and ranging radar were removed. The T.8C had TACAN and retained the cannon and radar. Some were later fitted with Harley lights (see Mk 11 section.). Later, three T.8s were converted to act as radar trainers for the new Blue Fox radar as fitted to the Sea Harrier; these became the T.8M and featured a sharply-pointed radome similar to that fitted to the Sea Harrier FRS.1.

With the introduction of the Avon 200-series F.6, Hawkers thought that a Series 200-powered trainer might attract greater export interest, especially in hot and high areas where the extra power would offer a useful safety margin. With that in mind,

readily distinguished by a large bulge on top of the nose to accommodate these. Painted in a striking white and green colour scheme, the aircraft ended up as a trials aircraft following cancellation of the TSR.2, working on various projects with the Royal Aircraft Establishment (RAE) at Farnborough, including early fly-by-wire experiments.

Mk 9

In the late-1950s, with the English Electric Lightning rapidly coming on-stream as the RAF's primary interceptor, the service had to decide what to do with the large numbers of Hunter F.6s in squadron service. As the role of overseas ground-attack fighter was then being filled by the obsolete de Havilland Venom, the answer was to convert the Hunter. Tropical trials for the Hunter were undertaken by two F.6 aircraft in Aden, the RAF concurrently evaluating the Gnat and Jet Provost for the same role; the result was a decisive win for the Hunter, and the decision was made to go forward with the conversion of 128 F.6s to the new FGA.9 standard.

Conceived as a tropicalised, ground-attack specialized version of the Hunter, the FGA.9 had a number of new features to optimize it for the role. As the aircraft was planned for service with the RAF's Near East, Middle East and Far East Air Forces, many of these experienced hot or high service conditions. More power was provided by the 10,050lb thrust Avon 207, while the carriage of the 230-gallon external tanks on the inner pylons was made standard by introducing a cutaway section on the flaps, and a bracing strut was fitted to

allow manoeuvring with the tanks fitted. To cope with the
increased weight, a braking parachute was fitted, housed in a
faired compartment above the tailpipe.

New external loads were cleared for use, and rocket
attachment points were fitted to the outer wings, straddling the
outer pylon position. Initially, up to 24 3-inch rockets could be
carried, but in later years, these were replaced by SNEB rocket
pods fitted directly to the outer pylons. 1,000lb bombs could
be fitted to the inner pylons, but as this precluded the carriage
of the 230-gallon fuel tanks and so severely cut into range,
these were rarely carried.

In the cockpit, a new gunsight and radio compass were
fitted. The aircraft had increased oxygen capacity, and the air
conditioning system was revamped to cope with the higher
ground temperatures of the tropics.

The new mark entered RAF service in early 1960, and was a
mainstay of overseas tactical support until the end of the
decade, later being used for weapons training into the 1980s.
The FGA.9 was also the standard to which many of the export
Hunters were rebuilt; not bad for a type that saw not one new-
build airframe!

Mk 10

In the late-1950s, the RAF's standard Fighter Reconnaissance
aircraft were the obsolete Meteor FR.9/PR.10, and the Swift
FR.5, which while a good platform, was dwindling in numbers
due to high attrition and fatigue. Hawkers had already
modified a single Hunter F.4 to carry a 5-camera nose as a
proof-of-concept prototype, but an F.6 with a 3-camera nose
would serve as the prototype for a production variant,

designated the FR.10. Fitted into a new nosecone were three
Vinten F.95 cameras (fitted either with 4- or 12-inch focal
length lenses); one was fitted facing forward and was protected
by eyelids when not in use, and the other two were mounted on
a bracket secured to the compartment's rear bulkhead, and
pointed to each side of the nose for oblique photography. The
cameras were staggered with the port camera mounted above
the starboard; this meant that their windows were set at
different heights.

Once again, 32 withdrawn F.6 airframes were taken in hand
for conversion, and the type emerged to a similar standard as
the FGA.9 with a new nose. In addition to the brake parachute
housing, the strengthened inner pylons, modified flaps and
more powerful engine of the FGA.9, the FR.10 had armour
plate fitted to the cockpit floor, and a cockpit voice recorder to
augment the wet film images.

Deliveries started in 1960; the FR.10 served with two RAF
Germany squadrons, and one flight in Aden, until replaced by
Hawker Siddeley Harrier GR.1s and McDonnell Douglas
Phantoms FGR.2s beginning in 1970. Many export nations
opted for small numbers of FR.10 analogs, and some former
RAF FR.10s were also sold on after withdrawal.

Mk 11

In early 1960, the Royal Navy issued a requirement for a
tactical weapons-training aircraft, and this need was met by
the conversion of 40 low-hour former-RAF F.4 airframes. Given
the designation GA.11, the aircraft retained the F.4's Avon 115
engine, compatible with the T.8 two-seater then in service with
the Fleet Air Arm (FAA).

All were fitted with the wing leading-edge extensions; though most retained the earlier two-pylon wing, 16 were fitted with the Mod 228 wing with four pylons. While these were wired for the Bullpup ASM and Sidewinder AAMs, those weapons were not used in service and usually each inner pylon carried a 100-gallon drop tank; practice bomb carriers or rocket pods would be fitted to the outer pylons of the Mod 228-winged examples.

The ADEN cannon pack was removed and the gun ports were faired over; the redundant gunsight was also removed, but the cockpit otherwise remained the same. An airfield

Export Hunters

While the specifics of Hunter exports are more fully explored in Chapter 3, it is worth a brief summary here.

The first export aircraft were standard F.4s for Belgium and the Netherlands. Most of these were licence-built and funded by the United States' Offshore Procurement Funding programme initiated in the mid-fifties. Other countries using the F.4 were Peru, Denmark and Sweden.

The Mark 6 was favoured by a number of other countries, including India and Switzerland, which received many new-build airframes, while some countries received refurbished

XF995 was built as an F.4 back in 1956, and converted to a T.8C in 1963. Now belonging to HHA, here she flies over Stonehenge in Wiltshire. *(© courtesy Mat Potulski/Hawker Hunter Aviation)*

An excellent study of an unidentified FGA.9 of 58 Squadron as it sits on the pan at Wittering. 58 only operated Hunters from 1973 to 78, and was a flight-strength advanced ground attack training unit
(© courtesy John Adams Collection)

arrestor hook was fitted, thought the Hunters were never intended to operate to carriers. Some Mk 11s were fitted with a large Harley light in the nose cone, this to aid optical tracking when operating as a sea-skimming anti-ship missile analog.

At least three Mk 11s were fitted with an FR.10 camera nose, and with this fitted were designated PR.11. An additional ventral camera port for a vertical camera was fitted to the otherwise standard FR.10 nose cone.

The first GA.11 conversion flew in January of 1962, and entered service with 738 and 764 Squadrons, FAA, shortly thereafter. These, along with other units, used the GA.11 until 1972 when most were retired. Around 20 were forwarded to FRADU, the Fleet Requirements and Air Direction Unit. This unit received its first GA.11s in 1969, and operated them until 1995, when the last were replaced by Hawks. Most, but not all, FRADU Hunters were fitted with the Harley light in the nose.

aircraft; this included Hunters for Lebanon, Jordan and Iraq.

The introduction of the FGA.9 for tropical/desert service spurred a new round of exports all based on a similar specification, with occasional special fits for specific countries. Many of these aircraft were airframes that had been bought by Hawkers specifically for rebuild, refurbishment or conversion. While most were retired Belgian or Dutch airframes, some were ex-RAF. More details can be found in Chapter 3.

The Hunter Today

The Hunter airframe has many virtues, being simple, strong and easy to operate, while possessing excellent performance. So it's no surprise that the type is still in demand for second-line military duties, and is popular as a warbird on the world airshow circuits. What may come as a surprise is the fact that one air force has taken steps to reintroduce the Hunter as a

front-line aircraft, albeit on what would seem to be a temporary basis. While a complete list of privately-operated Hunters would take up much space, and be necessarily subject to frequent change, here is a brief summary of the most important organizations still flying the Hunter:

Hawker Hunter Aviation

In December 2006, the Hunter re-entered RAF service in the form of 2 ex-Swiss F.58s leased from Hawker Hunter Aviation to act as targets for a SAM program; these were allocated RAF serials ZZ190 and ZZ191. They were followed by a T.7 in April 2007, this reverting to its original RAF serial, XF995. Based at RAF Scampton, Hawker Hunter Aviation is the largest operator of former military jet aircraft in Europe. It offers private sector outsourcing of realistic, high speed aerial threat simulation and mission support training services to the British Armed Forces and other defence contractors.

HHA started in the mid-80's as a partnership between the late Mark Hanna, former RAF pilot and the operator of warbirds with The Old Flying Machine Company (OFMC), and Mat Potulski, a successful management consultant in London. They began to explore the business opportunities for a fast jet squadron operated commercially under contract to armed forces in a variety of support roles - such as research and trials flying, aggressor training, and target towing, and thereby releasing front-line aircraft from second-line duties that eat into shrinking funds and aircraft fatigue life.

HHA looked at a number of types, including the Aero L-39/59, BAE Systems Hawk, Dassault-Breguet Alpha Jet, Douglas A-4 Skyhawk and North American F-100 Super Sabre, evaluating them on grounds of both absolute performance and through-life costs.

At that time, the Swiss government had decided to retire its Hunter fleet and HHA, through OFMC, purchased 12 single-seat Mk 58s, and obtained hangar space at the former RAF base at Scampton. The Hunter offers viceless handling, excellent subsonic performance, near-perfect reliability (over 98% on task serviceability) and good internal and external payload. In addition to the F.58s, HHA operates 2 two-seaters, a T.7 and a T.8. These aircraft are all low-houred and have been superbly maintained, so HHA expects to continue using them well into the late 2010s.

Lebanese Air Force

In 2008, Lebanon's new administration looked to strengthen its central authority over the various militias operating in the country. As part of the overhaul of the country's armed forces, there has been a revival of the neglected Lebanese Air. To this end, the LAF has pulled at least 6 Hunters from storage and is in the process of returning them to operational service, including at least one T.66 2-seater and the rest made up of F.70 single-seaters. These aircraft are drawn from the 8 Hunters which have been in storage at the Riyak AB since the mid-1990s, and which include 6 FGA.70s and 2 T.66s.

It appears that the LAF is operating the Hunters as an interim measure pending the delivery of 6 to 8 Hawk trainers/light fighters donated by the United Arab Emirates Air Force (UAEAF) and apparently, Lebanese pilots are being trained in the UAE to this end.

Northern Lights

Northern Lights is a Canadian company that provides various training support missions using the Hunter, flying high-speed attacks and missile simulations, target towing and providing realistic adversaries for ships and aircraft, while also operating various on-board electronic warfare (EW) training equipment.

These Hunters, flown by experienced former fighter pilots, are specially-modified and upgraded former Swiss Air Force F.58 airframes; the Hunters are IFR-certified and have been upgraded with various cockpit modifications, including dual Global Positioning Systems (GPS) and an Electronic Horizontal Situation Indicator. This provides the pilot with tremendous situational awareness about his position and all aircraft, ships and targets within the operating area thanks to electronic moving maps. They also carry up to 2 UHF and 3 VHF radios, as well as a TACAN, enabling the Hunters to integrate into any military operation. Furthermore, they can operate with Radar Warning Receivers, chaff/flare dispensers and are capable of carrying EW and ACMI pods as well as live-fire target-towing pods.

The Hunters are normally configured for EW missions with 4 external fuel tanks plus a combination of EW pods, including jammers and threat emitters, as well as ACMI. Depending on the mission profiles, this normally permits between 1.5 and 2.5 hours of on-station training time, plus the transit to and from the training area. Target towing, simulated attack, interception and other mission profiles allow for flights of 2 to 3 hours, depending on the requirements. The Hunters provide

ZZ191, a former Swiss F.58 now operated by Hawker Hunter Aviation on contract to the RAF, pictured here in 2007 (© courtesy Mat Potulski/Hawker Hunter Aviation)

Typical British airshow weather... F.6 XE557 seen here in 234 Squadron markings when the unit was a shadow squadron for 229 OCU in the 1960s and 70s. Note the triple-tier rockets under the wings and the selection of stores in front of the aircraft (© John Adams Collection)

Northern Lights with a combination of high speed, long endurance and potential configurations, combined with easy maintenance and good reliability. They are expected to remain in service for many years.

Thunder City

Brainchild of entrepreneur Mike Beachyhead, Thunder City offers flight experiences in ex-military aircraft including the English Electric Lightning, Blackburn Buccaneer and the Hunter. Thunder City has a total of seven Hunters, including both single- and two-seaters. The organization is based in South Africa where the less-restrictive civil aviation authorities allow all these aircraft types to fly on the airshow circuit and with passengers.

Delta Jets

Delta Jets was originally formed at Wellesbourne Mountford airfield to purchase and operate a former RAF Hunter, WV318/G-FFOX; in March 1996 it moved from there to

Kemble airfield, where they occupy the hangar used by the Red Arrows between 1967 and 1983.

Since the company's formation in 1995 Delta Jets has grown to be an expert in both the restoration and operation of classic British military jet aircraft, including the Hunter, Folland Gnat and BAC Jet Provost; in addition, Delta was granted maintenance and design authority over the Hunter in 1997. Delta also has the necessary clearance to maintain and restore Avon 100 and 200 engines.

Flying is undertaken by current or ex-military fast jet pilots, including Red Arrows, test pilots and air display pilots. Delta offers individuals and groups, with little or no flying experience, the chance to be able to fly in these historic aircraft. The jets can also be seen at air shows throughout the UK.

Delta Jets is registered with the Civil Aviation Authority as both a flight training and engineering organisation. The company's expertise and knowledge base, and its reputation for safe maintenance and operation of classic British jets, has subsequently appealed to a number of other operators, who

Despite appearances these three Hunters are all F.58s, now belonging to Northern Lights out of Canada. The closest two aircraft are C-GJMQ and –GIVX respectively (© courtesy Steve Legassick/Northern Lights)

One of Hawker's development aircraft, XG131 is shown here at Farnborough sporting wingtip tanks for trials – ultimately unsuccessful – and an impressive array of weaponry. Note the Short Seamew in the background – the contrast in grace could hardly be greater! (© Mark Gauntlett Collection)

now choose to entrust their private or syndicate-owned Hunters to Delta's care. Amongst their customers are Air Atlantique and the Royal Jordanian Historic Flight.

Additionally, Delta Jets now owns and operates three Hunters. These are all T.7s:
- XL577, painted in Blue Diamonds colours;
- WV318, painted in Black Arrows colours;
- WV372, painted in her original 2 Sqn camouflage colour scheme.

These are available for conversion training and for air experience flights.

With the popularity of the Hunter on the British airshow circuit, it is likely that Delta Jets will be operating for many years.

Experiments and Proposed Developments

The versatile Hunter airframe was subject to many experimental trials, and the development potential was such that Hawkers proposed a number of interesting follow-ons, none of which were to actually see the light of day. The F.1s used for acceptance trials and the unique T.12 have already been mentioned; additionally, an F.4, XF310, was used in trials of the Fairey Blue Sky AAM, which would later enter service as the Fireflash on the Lightning, and the third production F.6, WW594 was similarly modified for trials of the de Havilland Blue Jay AAM, that later became the Firestreak. This aircraft was designated P.1109A. Another F.6, XF378, undertook Firestreak firing trials over the Llanbedr ranges in Wales in 1957; this was known as the P.1109B. All of these airframes had modified noses for fire-control radar units associated with these missiles.

F.6 XG131 was modified to carry wingtip fuel tanks; this would have freed the wing pylons for carriage of other stores However, the tanks led to buffeting and were not adopted, XG131 being returned to standard configuration and delivered to the RAF. Another F.6, XF833, was delivered to Miles Aircraft at Shoreham in 1956 to be fitted with a Rolls-Royce thrust reverser – in the end, the familiar brake parachute was deemed a quicker fit and adequate for the task.

In addition to these actual airframes, a number of advanced paper aeroplanes were designed to extend the Hunter's capabilities. One of the first, in 1952, was the P.1083, a supersonic Hunter with a much-modified 'thin' wing with an increased sweepback of 50 degrees and an advance Avon RA.19R with afterburner – as it was, the project was cancelled in 1953 with the prototype 80% complete, and aside from the unique F.3, no Hunter received an afterburning engine. The unfinished fuselage was used to develop the F.6.

The issue was that the airframe was truly subsonic, and no amount of thrust would push a standard Hunter airframe through the sound barrier; supersonic speed was considered a necessity on 1950's fighter aircraft. A modified wing would make all the difference, hence the P.1083, mentioned above, and the P.1090 that featured the 50 degree P.1083 wing coupled with an extended fuselage to accommodate the big de Havilland Gyron engine, also with afterburner. This design required enlarged intakes as well to accommodate the vastly increased airflow requirements of the Gyron. A further extension of this thinking was the P.1091, which substituted a delta wing. However, the rate of airframe and engine development in the late 1950s meant that these designs were rapidly overtaken by aircraft designed from scratch, and no metal was ever cut.

One of the more interesting Hunter derivatives was the P.1128. This was a design for a six-seat light jet transport, with two Bristol Orpheus jets mounted in the rear fuselage, retaining the basic wings and tail section of the Hunter.

LIST OF HAWKER PROJECTS RELATED TO THE HUNTER	
P.1067	Day fighter to specification F.3/48. Became Hunter
P.1076	Development of P.1067
P.1083	Hunter with 50-degrees swept thin-wing
P.1090	Hunter with D.H. Gyron engine
P.1091	Hunter with delta wing and Gyron engine
P.1095	P.1083 with larger fuselage and Sapphire 4 or Avon RA.14, and reheat
P.1097	P.1083 with R.B.106
P.1099	Hunter with Avon RA.19 or RA.28 (became F.6)
P.1100	Supersonic development of Hunter with Avon R.A.24 and two rockets
P.1101	Two-seat Hunter trainer (became T.7)
P.1102	Hunter with new thin wing
P.1105	Hunter F.6 with podded rocket boost-engines
P.1106	Hunter with thin, greater span wing
P.1109	Hunter F.6 with Firestreak missiles
P.1114	All-weather 2-seat Hunter with Rolls-Royce Avon engine
P.1115	All-weather 2-seat Hunter with Armstrong-Siddeley Sapphire engine
P.1118	Supersonic Hunter with thin, straight wing
P.1120	Hunter advanced trainer
P.1128	Six-seat light transport jet with two Bristol-Siddeley Orpheus, based on Hunter
P.1130	Hunter two-seat, all-weather fighter
P.1133	Hunter with AI.23 radar and Firestreak missiles

A number of radar-equipped derivatives of the two-seat Hunter were also proposed for use in the night/all-weather interceptor role; these included the P.1114, P.1115, and P.1130. Some of these two-seat designs featuring a tandem seating arrangement rather than the familiar side-by-side layout adopted for the T.7.

In the late 1950s, the Central Fighter Establishment (CFE) proposed an advanced Hunter based on their experiences bringing the Hunter into service. The 'CFE Hunter' as it was known, would have had only two cannon but a larger ammunition supply; a non-afterburning Avon 301 powerplant, as used on the Lightning, or a Rolls-Royce Spey turbofan; a fuselage stretch to permit a greater fuel capacity; a drag chute and arresting hook; a new navigation system; and Sidewinder missiles.

In the end, the government's conviction that the concept of the manned military aircraft was dead consigned these paper designs to the wastebasket. Hawker abandoned Hunter development after the FGA.9 and concentrated on the new field of jet vertical take-off, starting with the P.1127, later developed as the Harrier.

The proposed P.1128 six-seat transport. Model by Chris Payne (© Chris Payne)

The Hunter in British Service

233 OCU Hunter F.1s parked at the eastern end of Pembrey's ASP (Aircraft Servicing Platform) in 1956. The unit was active with the Hunter for less than 18 months *(© Ted Gauntlett)*

Fighter/Ground Attack

The first production Hunter, WT555, flew in May 1953 and was the first Hunter to be delivered to an RAF unit, in this case, the Central Fighter Establishment based at RAF West Raynham. Experience soon highlighted a number of problems with the type as outlined in the previous chapter, and it wasn't until July 1954 that the first frontline RAF squadron was equipped with Hunters. This was No.43 Sqn, based at RAF Leuchars in Scotland and the Hunter replaced the outdated Gloster Meteor F.8. 43 was followed by 222 Sqn in December 1954 and 54 Sqn in February the following year, along with No.229 OCU.

With the F.2 equipping 257 Sqn (Sept. 1954) and 263 Sqn (Feb. 1955), the RAF had five operational Hunter squadrons, but these were subject to many restrictions due to inadequacy of the type and it is fair to say that the Hunter was not an effective fighter at this time. It was not until the F.4 and F.5 started to replace the earlier marks that the Hunter could truly be called an effective frontline aircraft. Due to the priority afforded the Hunter, and early recognition of the issues, this process began very quickly with No.98 Sqn being re-equipped with the F.4 starting in March 1955.

The majority of Hunter F.4s were assigned to the 2nd Tactical Air Force (2TAF), later known as RAF Germany, replacing the stop-gap North American Sabre and outmoded de Havilland Venom. In all, 13 RAF Germany squadrons operated the F.4 (Nos. 3, 4, 14, 20, 26, 67, 71, 93, 98, 112, 118, 130, 234 Sqns.), forming wings of 2 or 3 squadrons each housed at the same base. Two aircraft from each base formed a

Another 229 OCU shadow squadron was 234, in whose markings XG211 is seen here at a late-1960s air display *(© courtesy John Adams Collection)*

Quick Reaction Alert (QRA) flight, ready to scramble at a moment's notice if Warsaw Pact aircraft violated West German airspace, with the rest of the squadron on 15-minute readiness; each squadron in the wing rotated this assignment.

In Britain, the F.4 replaced the Meteor F.8 and re-equipped Hunter F.1 units, so that by early 1956, Nos. 43, 54, 66, 92, 111, 222, 245 and 247 Sqns of Fighter Command were using the F.4 and the contemporary F.5 was being used by a further five squadrons, Nos. 1, 34, 41, 56 and 263. This would all change very rapidly with the coming of the 1957 Defence White Paper that slashed Britain's defence budget and led to the disbandment of large numbers of squadrons just as the F.6 was beginning to enter service. The paper also predicted the demise of the manned fighter, to be replaced by ground-to-air missiles as Britain's primary defence system.

Ten UK-based and nine RAF Germany Hunter squadrons were disbanded; in addition, the plan to re-equip the Royal Auxiliary Air Force with Hunters was scrapped as the organization was stood down. The White Paper also cut expenditures on existing defence contracts, leading to the cancellation of 100 Hunter F.6 aircraft.

With the Lightning firmly established in service and the number of fighters in service declining, the Hunter was rapidly withdrawn from service in the interceptor role, but with the withdrawal of the F.6 came conversion to the FGA.9, and this aircraft in turn rapidly replaced the Venom and other types in service as ground-attack aircraft. Even so, numbers were but a fraction of those at the height of the F.4/5 era, and only seven frontline RAF squadrons were equipped with the mark. At home, No. 1 Sqn was re-equipped in January 1960, while the Middle East Air Force (MEAF) saw 8 Sqn stand up on the FGA.9 in the same month. Shortly thereafter Nos. 54 in the UK, 208, and 43 in the MEAF, and 20 and 28 Sqns in the Far East Air Force (FEAF) all switched to the versatile mark.

At the same time, the FR.10 was replacing the Meteor and Swift with 2 and 4 Sqns, with a small number also serving with 1417 Flight in Aden, but the Hunter force was now on the decline as the RAF transformed itself into a leaner organization focused on a European outlook. By the late sixties, the numbers of frontline Hunters had dwindled

Hunter F.1s of 233 OCU. at an unidentified station, possibly Tangmere or Leconfield, wearing Operation Vigilant markings, May, 1957. WT625 is visible in the foreground, which met its end at the Catterick Fire School in 1965
(© Ted Gauntlett)

79 Squadron was a shadow squadron of 229 OCU and two of its aircraft, XF435 and XG151, are seen in formation in 1971, just prior to the change in national markings. Both spent their whole careers with the RAF
(© courtesy John Adams Collection)

dramatically, and the last units, 1 and 54, converted to the Harrier and Phantom in 1969.

This wasn't quite the end of the line for Hunters in the front-line, as in 1972 there was a need for post-TWU refresher training for pilots waiting to be assigned to the newly-forming Jaguar squadrons. Two undersized squadrons were re-formed, the first being 45 Sqn, the other 58 Sqn which stood up in 1973. Based at RAF Wittering, the units' existence was short and they were disbanded in 1976 as the Jaguar force was brought up to full strength.

Training

However, the Hunter was too good an aircraft to discard altogether and many served with distinction with various training units, starting very early in the Hunter's career when F.1s were still being introduced into operational service. In fact, 229 OCU received its first Hunters as early as February 1955, and its first conversion course started in May of that year, beginning a span of almost 20 years in which it would operate Hunters. The unit initially operated around 25 Hunters alongside its Vampires; students initially flew the Vampire T.11 then graduated to the Vampire FB.5 for tactical flying training before conversion to the Hunter for about 20 hours of advanced tactical training. 229 OCU used various marks of Hunter until it was renamed the Tactical Weapons Unit in 1974.

Flying out of RAF Brawdy, the TWU consisted of three 'shadow' squadrons: 63, 79 and 234. 79 was responsible for refresher and weapons instructor training, while 63 and 234

both ran much longer operational training and weapons instruction courses for students fresh out of advanced flying training with 4 Flying Training School (4FTS). In 1978, the TWU was split into two sections, 1TWU which continued to use the Hunter out of Brawdy, while 2TWU transitioned to the British Aerospace Hawk T.1 and moved to Chivenor. 1TWU's Hunters were concentrated into 79 Squadron until replacement by Hawks in 1985.

Two other OCUs used the Hunter. One was 233 at Pembrey briefly in 1956-7 to assist with the large influx of aircrew converting to the Hunter, but it was with 237 OCU that the Hunter saw out its long RAF career. 237 was the Buccaneer Operational Conversion Unit, but as no dual-control trainer version of the Buccaneer was produced, the unit used modified Hunter T.7s for conversion and continuation training. The Hunters had some Buccaneer instrumentation fitted, including the Inertial Navigation System (INS) and were given the unofficial T.7D designation. In addition to the T.7Ds, the unit also used a variety of Hunters during 1980-81 when the Buccaneer was suddenly grounded following two fatal accidents involving catastrophic structural failure. Some 34 Hunters were taken from storage and borrowed from other units; the majority were two-seaters, but some F.6s and FGA.9s were also used. These aircraft were used to keep pilots and navigators current for around a year while the Buccaneers were inspected, repaired and returned to service. Most were then returned to storage or their units, but the specially-modified T.7s were retained right up until the final retirement of the Buccaneer in 1994.

F.4 XF994 at RAF Syerston, circa 1956. Shown serving with the Air Fighting Development Squadron, she was later converted to a T.8B, and in 1995, was the last FRADU Hunter to carry out an operational sortie. She is currently displayed at the Boscombe Down Museum *(© courtesy John Adams Collection)*

XE597 of 79 Squadron at Brawdy in 1983. While the a/c was scrapped in 1992, the cockpit section is extant *(© Mark Gauntlett Collection)*

One other training unit used Hunters. This was No.4 Flying Training School (4 FTS), which used a number of T.7s to supplement its Folland Gnats. Because the Gnat was small with a cramped cockpit, taller pilots were unable to train on it, and the larger Hunter was drafted in. Hunters were also used to train foreign pilots passing through the RAF training syllabus; often, these pilots would end up flying Hunters in their own country. The Hunters were used from 1967 until 1976, when they were again replaced by Hawks.

Other Service Units

With its easy handling and good performance, the Hunter was a natural trials and test aircraft, and many smaller service units had at least one on their roster over the course of the type's career.

The first of these was the Aeroplane and Armament Experimental Establishment (A&AEE) at RAF Boscombe Down, which received WB195, the second prototype, in December 1952 for initial trials. It was followed by many of the initial production aircraft as Hawkers and the RAF attempted

XE601 was a long-serving A&AEE Hunter, and is pictured here at Oerland, Norway, during trials. The tank under the inner pylon is a spray tank for chemical weapons training *(© courtesy John Adams Collection)*

Seen here at her base at West Raynham, F.1 WT680 served with the Day Fighter Leaders School from 1954 to 57. She is currently at the Anglia Hotel in Hargate, Lincs. in FGA.9 markings
(© Mark Gauntlett Collection)

The Central Flying School used many Hunters over the years, including this F.4 XF944. This aircraft was later converted to an F.58 for the Swiss *(© Mark Gauntlett Collection)*

A great period photo showing a scruffy-looking F.4 XF969 of the Empire Test Pilots School (ETPS) at Farnborough during airshow week. Note the faded or repainted areas on the fin and tailplanes and around the fuselage under the tailplane – replacement parts from another aircraft, possibly? Shame that she wasn't invited to the party!
(© Mark Gauntlett Collection)

to iron out the serious issues facing the Hunter at the start of its service life. The A&AEE operated many Hunters over the years on many different trials. The final Hunter on their books was T.7, WV383, named Hecate, Lady of the Night, which served as a night-attack avionics test-bed until 1998, when she was grounded due to a lack of funding to carry out a required major overhaul.

The Central Fighter Establishment (CFE) was another early user, receiving its first Hunter in July 1954. Based at West Raynham, the CFE included the Air Fighting Development Squadron (AFDS) and the Day Fighter Leader School (DFLS). Some of the Hunters used by the DFLS were amongst the most colourful of RAF Hunters. A Flight painted the spines, fins and tailplanes of their Hunters in red, with chord-wise bands around the wings, while B Flight used yellow.

The Fighter Weapons School used Hunters from 1956, eventually being absorbed by the CFE in 1958. Another central training unit was the Central Flying School that used an F.4 and T.7 between 1955 and 1963. Their task was to train flying instructors.

Another short-lived user was the Harrier Conversion Unit, which had a handful of FGA.9 aircraft for chase duties; as there were no Harrier two-seaters at the time, instructors would fly in formation with Harrier student pilots. These Hunters had the unit's small yellow grasshopper badge painted on the nose.

A long time Hunter user was the Empire Test Pilots School, starting in the mid-fifties and not retiring its last Hunter until 1999. Operating various single- and two-seat Hunters from Farnborough and Boscombe Down, in later years these were graced by the red, white and blue 'Raspberry Ripple' paint scheme.

The Royal Aircraft Establishment used a number of Hunters for various trials and experimental flying, including the sole Mk 12 XE531, in her glossy green and white colour scheme.

Aerobatics

As mentioned elsewhere, the Hunter had its shortcomings as a combat aircraft, but its handling characteristics were such that squadrons immediately started to form aerobatic teams – indeed, 54 Sqn with its F.1s appeared at the 1955 SBAC Airshow at Farnborough, representing No. 11 Group, Fighter Command. The formation became No. 54 Squadron Aerobatic Team in August 1955 and was unofficially known as 'The Black Knights' as the pilots dressed in black flying suits; they quickly gained international recognition and often performed at Official State Visits. The Aerobatic Team performed before their largest audience ever at the RAF Biggin Hill 'At Home' Day on September 17th, 1955 when, according to the Squadron's

Operational Record Book (ORB), for the very first time, the display 'was transmitted to the outside public via the magic eye of the television cameras'!

Another early Hunter aerobatic team were the Fighting Cocks of 43 Squadron, who formed a four-man team in 1956, though no special markings were applied to their aircraft. As worthy as these teams were, it was the exploits of two other squadrons that would capture the public's imagination on the world airshow scene. The first of these was 111 Sqn, which traded its Meteor F.8s for the Hunter F.4 in June 1955, and

111 Squadron displays at the Farnborough Airshow – note the Scimitars of 807 NAS awaiting their turn
(© Mark Gauntlett Collection)

Another ETPS Hunter, this time F.6 XF375 in a striking red and white colour scheme; note also the black cheat line stretching from the nose. She has been fitted with an instrumentation probe on the nose
(© courtesy John Adams Collection)

formed an aerobatic team shortly thereafter. This four-aircraft team was known at the Black Arrows; initially, the aircraft were flown in their standard camouflage. In 1957, 111 re-equipped with the F.6 and was chosen to be Fighter Command's aerobatic team. The team expanded to nine aircraft, each equipped with smoke generators and now painted overall gloss black. For the 1958 Farnborough Show, Treble One put up 14 of its own black-painted aircraft, then added a further 8 aircraft from 56 Sqn to perform one of the most famous aerobatic performances, a 22-aircraft loop that is still a world record.

111 relinquished its role in 1961 when it re-equipped with English Electric Lightnings, and it was 92 Sqn that took up the mantle with their Hunters. Performing as the Blue Diamonds, the team used up to 17 F.6 and one T.7, all painted gloss dark blue, a slightly paler shade than Roundel Blue. 92 was the official Fighter Command team for just two years, as after the 1962 airshow season the squadron started converting to the Lightning. 74 Squadron, equipped with the Lightning F.1A since 1960, became the new aerobatic team and marked the end of the Hunter's career as the RAF's preferred aerobatic aircraft.

Fleet Air Arm Service

The Fleet Air Arm operated about 80 Hunters in various training roles, starting with the T.8 in 1958, and receiving the single-seat GA.11 from 1962. The only frontline squadrons to operate Hunters were No.800 and 899 Sqns, which used a handful of T.8s as transitional trainers for the Buccaneer and Sea Harrier respectively; those operated by 899 had the Sea Harrier's Blue Fox radar fitted in an extended nose, and were designated the T.8M.

The first GA.11 conversion flew in January of 1962, and entered service with 738 and 764 Squadrons, FAA, shortly thereafter. 738 operated in the weapons training role, and at one point, the instructors formed an aerobatic team named the Rough Diamonds. The squadron was decommissioned in 1970.

764 offered air warfare instructor training and refresher courses for those returning to fast jet flying. The squadron was disbanded in 1972. GA.11s were also operated by 700 and 736 Squadrons.

The naval unit most famously associated with the Hunter was FRADU, the Fleet Requirements and Air Direction Unit. As the Royal navy's fixed-wing aircraft carriers were withdrawn from service in the 1970's and the Fleet Air Arm was run down, the Hunters were gradually retired. However, many of these aircraft gained a new lease of life with FRADU. Its tasks included assisting ships of the Royal Navy that were working up to operational standards, providing visual and radar tracking of aerial targets.

The unit received its first GA.11s at Hurn Airport near Bournemouth, in March 1969, initially alongside Scimitars, and operated up to 20 Hunters until 1995, when the last were replaced by Hawks. During this period, the unit formed an aerobatic team, the Blue Herons, perhaps the first civilian jet aerobatic team in the world, and they performed many displays between 1975 and the mid-80s. Most, but not all, FRADU Hunters were fitted with the Harley light in the nose, but FRADU also used the PR.11.

Mention should also be made of the three T.8s that were operated by Flag Office Flying Training (FOFT); flying from Yeovilton, these sported eye-catching gloss Roundel Blue over White colours.

Seen here with markings to commemorate the 40th Anniversary of the Hunter in 1991, T.8 XF357 looks very smart in her flat black scheme, originally painted to mark the retirement of ACM Sir Patrick Hine, a former Black Arrows leader
(© via Andy Evans)

A new use for an old airframe! XG194 masquerades as a Sukhoi Su-7 – most likely for use as an airfield decoy at the Electronic Warfare Range at RAF Spadeadam. The airframe is seen at North Luffenham
(© John Adams Collection)

Export Customers

The Hunter was one of the most successful British aircraft exports of all-time, finding employment with 20 air forces in addition to its service with the RAF and FAA. Export orders for the Hunter can be divided into two phases – new-build and licence-build contracts, and the rebuild and conversion of existing airframes for resale.

Interest was shown in the Hunter right at the outset, when Australia was looking to licence-build a modern jet fighter in 1950. Interest first settled on the P.1081, but when this was cancelled, the Australian Government looked at the Hunter. Events in Korea, where the RAAF's Meteor F.8 was thoroughly outclassed by the MiG-15, hastened a decision and as the Hunter would not be available within the specified timeframe, the Australians opted for an Avon-powered, licence-built version of the F-86 instead (As it was, the Avon Sabre didn't enter service until 1954). The first firm commitment was from Holland and Belgium, who signed a contract to licence-build the Hunter in May 1954. Further orders for aircraft built by Hawkers were placed by Sweden and Denmark in June and July 1954 respectively.

The major breakthrough in Hunter exports came when the Dutch and the Belgians set up a joint licence-production arrangement, involving Fokker in Holland and Avions Fairey and SABCA in Belgium, that produced a total of 445 machines, Fokker built all the Dutch machines and some of the Belgian machines; all Belgian production went to the Belgian Air Force. In the mid-sixties, many of these Dutch and Belgian aircraft were bought back by Hawkers for refurbishment or re-manufacture and onward export, generally brought up to the latest FGA.9 standard, or converted to two-seaters. This buy-back would play a major part in the revitalization of the Hunter export programme – while the number of former-RAF Hunters was relatively limited, these provided a good supply of aircraft that were refurbished and resold to many countries at relatively low cost. Aircraft for export were given sequential mark numbers, although equipment standards were generally the same. These are listed in the accompanying table.

The following is a brief summary of the Hunter's service with each export nation, listed in alphabetic order:

Abu Dhabi

An order for seven FGA.76s was placed in February of 1969 and delivered in November 1970. These were the first non-transport aircraft to serve with the then-Abu Dhabi Army Air Wing (Later Abu Dhabi Air Force), and serialled 701 to 707, formed their first ground-attack squadron based at Sharjah. At the same time, three FR.76A recon a/c (708-710) and two T.77 trainers (711 and 712) were ordered. As was often the case in the Middle East, the unit was initially manned by seconded RAF personnel, local pilots being trained in time to replace them. The Hunter's primary operational role was that of border patrol, during a long-running but low-intensity border dispute with Saudi Arabia.

The Hunters were supplanted in the interceptor role by Mirage 5s in 1974, but continued in the ground-attack role. They were replaced by BAe Hawks in 1983, and the surviving aircraft were gifted to Somalia.

Belgium

Along with the Netherlands, Belgium placed an order for Hunters in May 1954, to be built by SABCA and Avions Fairey. These were funded under the US offshore weapons procurement program and consisted of 111 Mk 4 and 96 Mk 6 aircraft, as well as 52 Mk 6s bought from Fokker and a single pattern aircraft provided by Hawkers to aid production. The first Mk 4s entered service in 1955, equipping nos. 1, 7 and 9 Wings at Beauvechain, Chievres and Bierset respectively. The Mk 6 started leaving the production lines in 1958, and gradually replaced the Mk 4s. As Belgium and the Netherlands shared flight-training facilities, Belgium did not acquire any two-seaters, relying on Dutch aircraft instead under a joint training programme.

The Belgian experience with the Hunter was not a happy one,

Belgian Air Force F.6 IF-13 of 7 Wing. Seen here at an airshow – note the USAF F-101 in the background – IF-13 was later converted to an Indian AF F.56A (A-463)
(© Mark Gauntlett Collection)

the Belgians claiming that the aircraft were of limited utility, unreliable and lacked spares, and these aircraft were little utilized before being replaced by the Lockheed F-104 Starfighter starting in the early 1960s; some were delivered straight to storage units, and when the airframes were bought by Hawkers in the late 1960s, they averaged only about 300 hours each, and rarely over 600, making them ideal candidates for refurbishment. Interestingly, the Dutch were much happier with their aircraft and kept them in service a lot longer.

While the Hunter was not universally popular in Belgian service, there was a notable exception. In 1956, Belgian Air Force (BAF) wings were locked in a competition to have an aerobatic team to represent Belgium at international airshows. The 7th Wing was chosen and training started. Their target was the 'Meeting of Nations' airshow, held in June 1957 at Bierset on the occasion of the Brussels Universal Exposition. NATO's best aerobatic teams, including the USAFE Skyblazers, La Patrouille de France, the 'Diavoli Rossi' of Italy, Britain's 'Black Arrows' (Also on Hunters) and teams from Greece, Turkey and Portugal. All of these teams had brightly painted aircraft, except the Belgians who performed with 5 aircraft painted in standard camouflage.

Following the meet, the team leader decided to have some aircraft painted with the Belgian colors under the wings for an airshow held in Chièvres in 1958. Although officially unapproved, the move was so popular with the public that BAF HQ later authorised 6 aircraft to be painted in a flamboyant Signal Red scheme and the all-red Hunters appeared for the first time in public on May 7th, 1960 at the Chaumont, France airshow. The team was also given a name – The Red Devils, or 'Les Diables Rouges/ De Rode Duivels' in French and Flemish, the two official languages of Belgium.

The team was very popular both at home and abroad, but due to the early withdrawal of the Hunter from front line units, the team performed their last show on Hunters on October 4th, 1963 in Chièvres. After two years disbandment, the Red Devils came back in 1965 in Fouga CM170 Magister training aircraft, but many still remember the red Hunters.

Chile

Chile was one of the largest buyers of Hunters, and one of the longest users. When negotiations with the US for F-86s broke down, the Chilean government turned to Britain for the Hunter; a superior aircraft in any case! Their initial order, in 1966, was

The clean lines of the early Hunters are emphasized by this Belgian F.4 ID-136. Built in mid-1957, she was destined for a very short life, being struck off charge and scrapped in 1960
(© WA Harrison Collection)

Indian AF A460 was a former Belgian F.4 converted to F.66A status in 1966. She is seen here during her delivery flight, probably at Malta
(© Mark Gauntlett Collection)

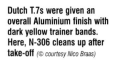

A trio of Chilean Air Force Hunter FGA.71s sandwich **FR.71A J-734** *(© courtesy FACh)*

for 15 FGA.71s and was rapidly followed by three T.72s and three FR.71As, which were the export equivalent of the FR.10. All of these were delivered to the Fuerza Aerea de Chile (FACH) in 1967-8, and equipped 7 Grupo at Los Cerrillos Air Base near the capital Santiago. Further deliveries in 1970-1 added 9 FGA.71s, and an additional four in 1973, plus three more FR.71As and two T.72s. These added airframes allowed the re-equipment of two more Grupos, No. 9 (Panteras Negras) at Puerto Montt and No. 8 at Cerro Moreno.

Chilean Hunters saw combat during the 1973 right-wing military coup that overthrew Marxist President Salvador Allende, bombing and strafing the presidential palace; following this coup and subsequent human rights violations of the new military government, Britain applied an arms embargo that stopped all support and spares deliveries. This led to Chile turning to other sources for combat aircraft, although they would probably have ordered more Hunters given the chance. As it was, numbers dwindled as unserviceable aircraft were cannibalized to keep a worthwhile number in the air, and remaining aircraft were concentrated on Grupo 8 by 1981 as other Grupos re-equipped with Northrop F-5Es.

Beginning in 1980, these remaining Hunters were given a home-grown upgrade, carried out by ENAER in Chile. Called

Programa Aguila (Eagle), this involved fitting the locally developed Caiquen Radar Warning Receiver (RWR) in a bullet fairing on the top of the fin, Eclipse chaff/flare dispensers, the ability to carry IAI Shafrir AAMs and other minor improvements mainly related to the improving the cockpit. Israeli assistance with this upgrade is rumoured.

A change of British government, and limited reforms by the Chilean government brought about a swansong in Chilean Hunter history, as historic border tensions between Chile and Argentina and the Falklands War led to the delivery of at least 12 FGA.9s from RAF stocks in 1981 and 1982; these were augmented by the delivery of spares for existing airframes and gave a major boost to Chilean airpower at a time when Argentina was weakened.

After years of faithful service, the inevitable obsolescence of the Hunter in the region began to show and replacement types were bought, including the Mirage V and F-16; all Chilean Hunters were retired by April 1995 following a flypast of the type over the capital. Many are on display at the Chilean Air Force Museum; one of the two-seaters, J-736, was sold to EMBRAER, the Brazilian commercial aircraft manufacturer, and is still in use as a chase plane.

Dutch T.7s were given an overall Aluminium finish with dark yellow trainer bands. Here, N-306 cleans up after take-off *(© courtesy Nico Braas)*

Denmark

Second to buy the Hunter directly from Hawker – Denmark did not have an indigenous jet aircraft manufacturing industry - Denmark's order for 30 aircraft was placed just four days after the Swedes', on July 3rd, 1954. These were identical to the RAF's F.4, and were designated F.51 by Hawkers. Deliveries began in January 1956 and finished in September that year, the Hunters replacing the Gloster Meteor F.4s and F.8s then in service with the Royal Danish Air Force (RDAF), or Kongelige Danske Flyvevabnet. In RDAF service, the aircraft were serialled E-401 to 430 and all served with Eskadrille 724 at Aalborg, and later Karup and Skydstrup. A total of 4 two-seat trainers were acquired, two new-build and two former Dutch aircraft, all to T.7 standard.

The aircraft were very popular with their pilots and had an excellent safety record – one Hunter suffered a flame-out on approach; the pilot ejected, but the aircraft landed itself with little damage and was repaired for service within a month. The Hunters were retired in March 1974 and sold back to Hawkers. Because they were so well-used, they were not suitable candidates for refurbishment and most were given to museums in Britain and Europe; many are still on display.

Holland

Along with Belgium, the Dutch were the first export customers for the Hunter, opting to licence-build the type at the Fokker factory. As with Belgium, these were funded by the US Government. Delivery of 96 Mk 4s started at the end of 1955, with serials starting at N-101. These replaced the Gloster Meteor and equipped nos. 323, 324 and 325 Squadrons, based at Leeuwarden, and 326 and 327 at Soesterberg. In 1957, production switched to the F.6, and 93 of these were delivered, these being serialled from N-201. 20 two-seat trainers were ordered in 1955, but these were delivered from Britain rather than being licence-built airframes.

Dutch Hunters were the first to be equipped with Sidewinder missiles, attached to shoes fitted to the outboard wing pylons, the inners being fitted with standard 100-gallon drop tanks. At least one F.4, N-113, was fitted with a modified drop tank that contained filters to extract radioactive particles from the atmosphere at high altitude.

While the Dutch Hunters did not see combat, they did deploy to potentially hostile airspace, when Indonesia started to make war-like noises about the Dutch colony on West Irian Jaya. In 1960, no. 322 Squadron was deployed to Biak Island in Dutch

N-301 was the first Dutch T.7, built by Hawkers in 1958. She later served with Abu Dhabi and Oman (© courtesy Nico Braas)

Denmark's Hunters were not suitable for refurbishing on retirement, so many were donated to museums across Europe. Here, E-421 is seen on display at the Brooklands Museum in 1995 (© Author)

New Guinea, staying there until the territory was diplomatically ceded to Indonesia in 1962.

The F.4s entered service in 1956, when they replaced the elderly Gloster Meteor F.8s in Koninklijke Luchmacht (KLu) service, and were retired in August 1963. The F.6s started replacing the F.4s in 1957, and these served on until August 1968, when they were replaced in turn by the Lockheed F-104. Many airframes were sold back to Hawkers for refurbishment and resale.

Interestingly, while the cartridge link collector tanks were nicknamed 'Sabrinas' in RAF service, they were known at 'Sophias' in Dutch service, for the actress Sophia Loren!

India

Involved in hostilities with neighbouring Pakistan since independence in 1948, India was an early Hunter operator, and also one of the longest as it didn't retire its last aircraft until 2000. Indian interest was indicated as early as 1954, when she asked for information and specifications for 100 aircraft, this at a time when the Mark 1 was proving problematic in RAF service. However, by 1956 an Indian Air Force (IAF) mission to Britain evaluated the aircraft and an order was placed the following year for 160 Hunters to F.6 standards and designated as F.56s; delivery of these began in October when the first of 32 aircraft originally ordered for the RAF but later cancelled were completed for India instead. 16 more were taken from RAF stocks and refurbished before delivery; the remaining 112, including 22 two-seat T.66s, were all new-build specifically to Indian standards.

These aircraft were used to equip seven squadrons: 7, 14, 27, 17, 20, 37 and 5. The T.66s were assigned to operational squadrons at this time; later, they would be concentrated in OCUs. These squadrons were to see action on many occasions, starting in 1961 when they covered the Indian occupation of Goa. The Hunter's involvement in the major Indo-Pakistan Wars

is covered in the following chapter.

In the aftermath of the 1965 war, India decided to expand the Hunter force having found the aircraft to be a rugged and reliable performer. Three large follow-on orders were placed, totaling some 53 single-seaters to FGA.9 standards, and 12 more T.66 trainers. A final batch of 5 T.66s was delivered in 1973, these being the last new Hunters received by India, bringing the grand total to 193 single-seat aircraft and 39 two-seaters. An unknown number of IAF Hunters were locally upgraded to FR.10 specifications with a camera nose.

Indian Hunters began to be replaced by the MiG-21 in the early 1970s in the fighter/interceptor role, and in the ground attack role by the locally-built SEPECAT Jaguar in the late 1970s, however the Hunter was to linger on in second-line roles for a long time, flying as advanced trainers and target tugs. The last IAF Hunter unit was the Indian Banners squadron, where some F.66 and T.66 airframes were used for target towing until 1999.

The Thunderbolts aerobatic team was formed in 1982 for the Golden Jubilee of the Indian Air Force. They flew nine Hawker Hunter F.56A airplanes as part of 20 Squadron, IAF. Each aircraft was painted dark blue with distinctive white lightning bolts painted on the fuselage and wings – looking at photos, it appears that no two patterns were exactly the same. The Thunderbolts were disbanded in 1990.

Iraq

Iraq's Hunters were amongst the most active, taking part in at least two wars and in other operations during a 30-year career. Their first 15 Hunters were drawn from RAF stocks and were unmodified F.6s, serialled 394 to 409, presented to the then-Hashemite Kingdom in late 1957. Soon after, the King was overthrown in an army coup, and an arms embargo restricted the delivery of support and spares until a more pro-western regime took over in 1963. During the following four years, Iraq ordered further batches of aircraft, all to FGA.9 standard: 24

In a surprise move, Lebanon has returned some of her Hunters to operational service. L-284 is shown in a hangar at Riyak Airbase
(© courtesy Lebanese Armed Forces)

FGA.59 in 1964, 18 FGA.59As in 1965, and four FGA.59B in 1966. In addition, 6 two-seat T.60s were delivered in 1964-5, Iraq having previously borrowed the much-travelled two-seat demonstrator G-APUX for a year on evaluation.

Following the 1967 Six-Day War, and the 1968 overthrow of the pro-western government by the socialist Ba'athist Party, support from Britain was withdrawn and no further sales, spares or support would be forthcoming.

Losses in 1967 and in the 1973 Yom Kippur War depleted the Iraqi Hunter fleet, but these were still active long into the seventies before being replaced in the front line by Sukhoi Su-7s. Still active in the operational training role into the 1980s, it is strongly rumoured that Iraqi Hunters were fitted with spray tanks on the wing pylons and used to spray nerve gas on Kurdish villages in the north of Iraq, and possibly also against Iranian troops in the long-running Iran-Iraq War.

Finally withdrawn from service in the late 1980s, the remaining Hunters were deployed on various Iraqi airfields as decoys, and during the 1991 Gulf War, at least one was the subject of a guided bomb attack captured on film by the US Air Force. It seems unlikely that any Hunters have survived in Iraq.

Jordan

With close ties to Britain, the Hashemite Kingdom of Jordan was a natural Hunter customer and the Royal Jordanian Air Force (RJAF) acquired a large number starting in 1958, when 12 ex-RAF F.6s were delivered to equip No.1 Squadron based at Mafraq. Three T.66B trainers were acquired in 1960, and these equipped No.6 Squadron as the Hunter OCU; the famous G-APUX was also used by this unit for a year on loan from Hawkers. Two ex-RAF FR.10s were also transferred to the RJAF at the same time. These were followed in 1962 by 12 FGA.9s, also from RAF stocks, which were used to form No 2 Sqn – these aircraft formed an aerobatic team, the Hashemite Diamond. King Hussein of Jordan, who was a skilled pilot, is believed to have checked out on the single-seat Hunter.

These Hunters were to see combat against the Israeli Air Force in 1964, becoming involved in border skirmishes and acquitting themselves very well against Mirage IIIs, claiming a number of kills. However, the Six Day War of 1967 dealt a serious blow to the Jordanian Hunter fleet, as most of them were

destroyed or seriously damaged in surprise attacks on their airfields. Their pilots flew with the Iraqi Air Force for the remainder of the war.

Following the war, the RJAF acquired replacement Hunters from a variety of sources; Saudi Arabia gifted three of their single-seaters, while 18 were ordered from Hawkers. These aircraft played no direct part in the 1973 Yom Kippur War, but remained on a defensive footing. Replacement came shortly thereafter as deliveries of F-5Es began in 1975; the remaining 31 Hunters were transferred to Oman.

Kenya

In 1974, the Kenyan Air Force took delivery of four FGA.80 and two T.81, serialled from 801 to 806, based at the then-new airfield at Nanyuki. Service in Kenya was short and the five survivors were placed in storage in 1979 then sold to Zimbabwe in 1981 following the delivery of F-5s.

Kuwait

Oil-rich Kuwait became independent of Britain in 1961 but her independence was challenged by Iraq, and Britain sent forces including RAF Hunters to the country to ensure her freedom. In 1965, the Kuwaiti government ordered four single-seat Hunters (FGA.57) to start its own air force. These refurbished aircraft were joined in 1967 by a further two ex-RAF F.6s and five T.67s, as well as a small batch of English Electric Lightnings that replaced the Hunters in the air defence role.

With the delivery of the Lightnings, the Hunters switched to ground-attack with a secondary fighter role, but were replaced by A-4 Skyhawks in 1976. The two-seaters remained as advanced trainers until they were put into storage in 1980. No Kuwaiti Hunters took part in the 1991 Gulf War, but one of the single-seaters is displayed at the Kuwaiti Air Force Museum.

Lebanon

Lebanon's first Hunters were 6 former RAF F.6s paid for with US Offshore Procurement funds in 1958, and these were augmented by the loan of Hawker's two-seat demonstrator G-APUX in 1963. When Hawkers recalled it, Lebanon placed an order for 3 T.66Cs and 4 FGA.70s, all converted from ex-Belgian F.6s and delivered in 1965-6. A distinguishing feature of the Lebanese Air Force

(LAF) Hunters was the large UHF blade aerial just aft of the canopy. A final order for 6 FGA.70s was placed in 1975; three were delivered immediately, but the others were delayed until a lull in the civil war in that country in 1977. Hunters served with 2nd Squadron and were based at Rayak (Sometimes Riyak) and Byblos (Halat), though the F.6s could not operate out of Byblos due to the shortness of the runway and the lack of a brake parachute, as carried by the FGA.70s.

Renewed fighting in the country in 1982-3 ensured that these aircraft would see combat service, but this was hampered by a lack of suitable weaponry, the Hunters relying on their cannon and on SNEB rockets, while a few 500lb bombs were also used. At least two were shot down and a further one badly damaged. This aircraft flew to Cyprus to prevent its home base being blocked; it was repaired there and returned to Lebanon shortly thereafter. Hunters were used sporadically into the early 1990s when the remaining aircraft were stored as the Lebanese armed forces concentrated on the use of helicopters.

With a fragile new administration in the Lebanon in 2008, the Armed Forces are looking to strengthen themselves to replace the militias across the country. Reliable reports indicate that the LAF has returned at least 6 Hunters to operational service, including at least one T.66 2-seater and the rest made up of F.70 single-seaters. These aircraft are drawn from the 8 Hunters which have been in storage at the Riyak AB since the mid-1990s, and which include 6 FGA.70s and 2 T.66s.

It is further reported that the LAF is operating the Hunters as an interim measure pending the delivery of 6 to 8 Hawk trainers/light fighters from the United Arab Emirates Air Force (UAEAF) which has apparently pledged to donate them to Lebanon in the near future; these reports also suggest that a number of LAF pilots have been undergoing training on these aircraft in the UAE.

Oman

Oman was a latecomer to the ranks of Hunter operators, receiving 31 aircraft as a gift from King Hussein of Jordan in 1975. These aircraft added a new dimension to the Sultan of Oman's Air Force (SOAF) that had previously operated nothing more warlike than the BAC Strikemaster armed trainer, though RAF Hunters had been based in the country on a regular basis. These were used to equip a full squadron, No. 6, at the brand-new Thumrait airbase, where British pilots and support personnel maintained around 16 of the aircraft, the others being used for spares recovery.

These aircraft were used to combat incursions by Marxist terrorists from neighbouring Yemen, using dumb bombs, rocket pods and the 30mm cannon. In the 1980s a number of aircraft were fitted with AIM-9P Sidewinders and defensive countermeasures systems. By 1993, only a handful of Hunters remained operational with the renamed Royal Air Force of Oman and these were retired late in that year, replaced by the Sepecat Jaguar and BAe Hawk.

Peru

One of the first Hunter export customers, Peru ordered 16 ex-RAF Mk 4, designated F.52, to supplement its F-86s. Operated by Escuadron de Caza (Fighter Squadron) 14 'The Fighting Roosters' at Talara and Limatambo, deliveries began in May 1956, and the aircraft were serialled 630 to 645. In March 1960, a single two-seater T.62, serialled 681, was delivered for conversion training. This was distinguished by a blister fairing aft of the cockpit containing a radio compass.

The pilots of Escuadron 14 formed an aerobatic team, The Four Aces, in September 1956 initially to celebrate Aviation Day in Peru. The team was famed for landing in a 'diamond four' formation.

Rapid advances in fighter technology saw the Hunters replaced by Mirage 5s in the interceptor role in 1968, being switched to ground attack with Escuadron de Caza 12. Despite having just the Mk 4's standard two wing pylons, the aircraft were well liked in this role, but were replaced by Sukhoi Su-22s in 1976. After a further switch to the advanced training role, the 10 surviving Hunters were finally retired in 1980.

Qatar

Qatar was the second of the Arabian Emirates to order the Hunter, following Abu Dhabi. Three FGA.78s (QA10 to 12) and one T.79 (QA13) were all refurbished and updated former Dutch airframes, and were delivered in 1971. They were operated by the quaintly-named Qatar Public Safety Force, later the Qatar Emiri Air Force, from the air base at Doha. As with many Hunter operators, they were flown and serviced by seconded RAF personnel, with a sprinkling of local crew being transitioned over time.

The Hunters were replaced by Dassault Alpha Jets in the mid-1980s. Two of these aircraft still survive in private hands in Britain. QA10 is displayed in its original Dutch colours at the Yorkshire Air Museum, Elvington, while the nose section and tail fin of QA12 are being restored by Mark Gauntlett in Wales.

Rhodesia/Zimbabwe

The Royal Rhodesian Air Force received 12 former-RAF F.6 aircraft in 1962-3; these had been converted by Hawker to FGA.9s and retained this designation, presumably as South Rhodesia remained a British colony at the time. Coded RRAF 116 to 127, the Hunters equipped No.1 Sqn and were based at Thornhill AFB near Gwelo. At the time, these aircraft were painted in the standard RAF camouflage colours. Later, this was modified to an overall Dark Brown with Dark Green disruptive camouflage on the upper surfaces.

With the Unilateral Declaration of Independence in 1965, Rhodesia was subject to economic and military sanctions, and British support for the Hunter fleet was terminated. Local modifications and help from fellow outcasts, South Africa, ensured that the Hunters remained a viable weapon; indeed many local modifications were carried out, and some aircraft were flown to South Africa, where they were fitted to carry AAMs. With the increase in violence by guerillas, the Hunter fleet was an important tool – simple, rugged and able to carry a powerful punch.

Following the long struggle, white minority rule ended in 1980, and Rhodesia became Zimbabwe. Although the majority of the white pilots and ground crew eventually left the country, the Hunter remained in service due to its relatively simple structure; indeed, numbers increased as Britain gifted 9 aircraft to the new Zimbabwe government, and 6 were bought from Kenya. These aircraft remained in standard RAF camouflage.

A sabotage attack on the Thornhill base in 1982 destroyed at least 8 Hunters, and the remainder were subject to a further embargo on the Mugabe regime; the Hunters dwindled in numbers as spares ran out and the handful of survivors were withdrawn from service in 2002.

Saudi Arabia

As part of a large defence package, named 'Magic Carpet', six Hunters were delivered to the Saudis in 1966 in order to ease the transition to the complex BAC Lightnings that were a major component of the contract. These Hunters were four refurbished F.6s (coded 60-601 to 604) and two T.7s (70-616 and 617). The Hunters were very much a transitional type for the Saudis and little use was made of them. One F.6 was lost in an accident in 1967, while the other three were gifted to Jordan following the 1967 Six-Day War. The T.7s were retained until 1974, when they were returned to the RAF.

Singapore

With British imperial commitments being run down in the 1960s, the Singapore government recognised the necessity of providing for their own defence rather than relying on British units that were being withdrawn rapidly. Singapore became an independent state in August 1965, and immediately began to set up its own armed forces, including an air element known as the Singapore Air Defence Command (SADC). In the light of Britain's 1968 statement regarding the withdrawal of its armed forces from the Far East by 1971, these plans were accelerated and in July 1968, an order for 20 refurbished Hunters was placed. The Hawker Hunter was the first jet fighter aircraft to enter service with the SADC (renamed the Republic of Singapore Air Force (RSAF) from 1975) and was to provide 22 years of sterling service.

This order included the purchase of 12 single-seat Hunter F.74s (basically FGA.9s), for dual day fighter/ground-attack role, four Hunter FR.74As (FR.10s) to provide a tactical reconnaissance element and four two-seat Hunter T.75 fighter trainers, similar to the T.7. The single-seat Hunters were powered by Rolls Royce Avon 207 engines and equipped with the larger 230 gallon drop-tanks, while the four T.75s were powered by Avon 122 engines and carried the smaller 100 gallon drop-tanks, with no provisions for the larger 230 gallon drop-tanks.

At first, Singaporean pilots were trained by the RAF in Britain, including a 24-week advanced training course on Hunters with 4FTS at RAF Valley, before a further 20-week operational conversion course at RAF Chivenor. Later, pilots were trained to basic standards in Singapore, before completing the advanced and conversion training in Britain.

Singapore's first two Hunters (500 and 504) arrived at Tengah

Saudi T.70 70-616 had an interesting life, starting in 1959 as an RAF T.7 with 66 and 74 Squadrons before being refurbished for service with the Saudis in 1966, as seen here at Hurn prior to delivery. In 1968, she was delivered to Jordan, before being sold back to the RAF in 1974 as XX466. She was transferred to the Royal Navy in 1984 for service with FRADU and finally retired in 1993. Unfortunately, this much-storied airframe was burned on a dump in 1996
(© Dave Smith)

air base in Singapore on July 14th, 1970; during the working-up period, the air defence of Singapore was entrusted to 74 Sqn, RAF, with their Lightnings. Following the return of the first batch of British-trained Hunter pilots, SADC's first operational fighter squadron, 140 (Osprey) Squadron, was formed on September 8th, 1970. The unit was commanded by Major Chris Strong, an RAF pilot with long experience on Hunters and who had been the Commanding Officer (CO) of RAF 20 Squadron, also flying Hunters, based at Tengah until it was disbanded in February 1970. Maj. Strong was asked by SADC to stay in Singapore as the first CO of 140 Squadron.

In 1971, a further 27 refurbished Hunters, consisting of 22 F.74Bs and five T.75As, were ordered to enable a second squadron to be formed. The F.74Bs differing from the basic F.74 only in having a Marconi AD370B radio compass. The T.75As differed from the T.75s primarily in that they had the more-powerful Avon 207 engine and the ability to carry the larger 230-gallon drop-tanks. Most of the single-seaters were wired to carry Sidewinder AAMs. Uniquely, some Singaporean Hunters were upgraded with a 'wet' centreline stores pylon for external fuel; this allowed carriage of bombs on the inner stores pylons, which would normally have been fitted with 230-gallon drop tanks. This modification was implemented with assistance from the Lockheed Corporation.

With these additional deliveries, 141 (Merlin) Squadron was formed on December 1st, 1972 with Maj. Royston Coleman, formerly RAF, as its first CO. The squadron's primary role was daytime air defence with a secondary role of supporting maritime and land forces.

By 1973, the Hunter squadrons were firmly established, and confidence in the aircraft was such that the Hunter Wing Aerobatics Team was formed in March of that year. The team, initially known as 'Osprey Red', was led by Maj. Strong, and staged its first practice on March 10th, 1973 and later performed at the 1973 SAF Day Display in July at Changi Air Base. Prior to the aerobatics display, 16 Hunters made a spectacular flypast in perfect diamond formation. As the pool of local Hunter pilots

grew larger and more experienced, an all-Singapore aerobatics team was formed for the first time in 1974. Called the 'Black Knights', the team had five Hunters and performed publicly for the first time at the SAF Day Display held at Changi Air Base in June 1974.

Reorganisation of the fighter squadrons in Tengah took place on 15 May 1981. 141 Squadron, which by this time operated both Hunters and A-4 Skyhawks, was disbanded and the remaining Hunters were centralised in 140 Squadron. After 12 years of operations in Tengah, 140 Squadron moved to Paya Lebar on 14 April 1983.

Meantime, the three 'small bore' trainers (500, 504 & 516) were withdrawn from service in December 1984, leaving just the large-bore T.74As in service.

By the late eighties, the Hunter was becoming rather long in the tooth, and the RSAF ordered the General Dynamics F-16A as its replacement. With the delivery of eight F-16A/B Block 15 Fighting Falcons in January 1990, the Hunters in 140 Squadron were re-assigned to 141 (Merlin) Squadron, which was re-formed on 8 February 1990. The Hunters continued to serve primarily in the reconnaissance role with 141 Squadron. With the ageing of the Hunter fleet and its impending retirement, a new reconnaissance platform had to be found; the RSAF converted eight of its F-5Es to RF-5E standard, the first being delivered to 141 Squadron in June 1991.

The Hunters were eventually retired on April 1992 with one last sortie consisting of five aircraft lead by Brigadier General Michael Teo, Chief of the Air Force, marking the end of 22 years of service with the RSAF. Of the remaining aircraft, three T.75As were used as ground instructional airframes, one (501) was mounted as gate guardian, one (519) displayed in the RSAF Museum and one displayed at the SAF Military Institute. The remaining 21 aircraft were later sold to an Australian company where many remain.

(With sincere thanks to LTC Goh Yong Kiat (RSAF) and Michael Ng Wee Hong (Singapore Ministry of Defence) for information and photos.)

Somalia

Despite being a long-standing Soviet client-nation led by Marxist President Siad Barre, Somalia also had close relations with many Arab nations, and in 1983, Abu Dhabi transferred some surplus military equipment to the Somali government. This package included 9 Hunters, comprised of 8 FGA.76s and FR.76As plus a single T.77 trainer. These were based at Berbera, an important deep-ocean port in north-west Somalia, and were flown and maintained by mercenaries, mostly from Zimbabwe and South Africa.

The Hunters were flown operationally against anti-government groups based in Ethiopia and remote areas of Somalia. Unconfirmed reports suggest that at least one of these aircraft was fitted with Soviet AA-2 'Atoll' AAMs, a copy of the Sidewinder.

When central government in Somalia collapsed in 1991, the air force fell apart and the Hunters were left to rot in their revetments. Recent photos of the aircraft show them in a severely dilapidated condition; it is unlikely that these aircraft will be repairable if central authority is restored.

Sweden

Sweden became the first export customer for the Hunter, signing a contract for 120 F.4 airframes on June 29th, 1954; these were designated F.50 by Hawkers and J.34 by the Flygvapnet (Swedish Air Force). The F.50s were serialled 34001 to 34120, and the first made its first flight on June 24th, 1955. No two-seaters were bought.

While built to the same standards as RAF F.4s, the F.50s initially lacked the prominent link collector tanks under the nose, though these were retro-fitted, and while they never received the dogtooth wing extensions, they were built with the Mod 288 four-pylon wing. However, Swedish Hunters were amongst the first to be fitted with Sidewinder air-to-air missiles, on rewired outboard wing pylons. A small number were fitted with a Volvo Flygmotor afterburner system, but this was not used operationally and with the Lansen and Draken coming online, no further modifications were attempted.

F.50s were flown by four Wings (F8, F9, F10 and F18) until being retired in 1966. F18 formed an acrobatic team named the Acro Hunters in 1962.

Switzerland

As an operator of the Vampire and Venom, Switzerland took a keen interest in the development of the Hunter, but as the indigenous FFA P-16 was then under development for the Swiss Air Force, the interest did not materialize into an order. However, the P-16 was cancelled after the two prototypes both crashed and a competition was set up to find a readily available interceptor/fighter-bomber. Amongst those evaluated were the F-86, MiG-15, Folland Gnat and Mystere IV, but it was the Hunter that came out head and shoulders above them all and an order for 100 Mk 58 airframes was secured in January 1958. The first 12 of the batch were ex-RAF F.6s, while the other 88 were new-build machines.

Though built to F.6 standards, these aircraft did feature the brake parachute housing seen on the T.7 and later the FGA.9 – this was necessary because of the short length of many of the landing strips used by the Swiss, including stretches of autobahn. Additionally, they carried Swiss radios, and strengthened outboard stores pylons that could carry 400 kilogram (880 pound) bombs. Deliveries started in 1959 to Fliegerstaffeln 1 and 11; they were followed by 5ieme Escadrille, and Fliegerstaffeln 8 and 21. The last three squadrons were manned by part-time reservists, who make up a good portion of the Swiss armed forces.

In 1970, Switzerland ordered the Vought A-7 as a replacement for its Venoms in the fighter-bomber role; as an interim measure, an additional 30 Hunters were purchased. When the full costs of the A-7 became apparent, the order was cancelled and a further 30 Hunters ordered, 8 of them T.68 two-seaters. The 22 F.58As were delivered in kit form and featured the Avon 207 engine, replacing the Avon 203 engine used in the original F.58 batch; the older F.58s were retrofitted with the Avon 207 at a later date. The trainers were fitted with twin Aden cannon. These additional aircraft allowed Fliegerstaffeln 4, 7, 18 and 19 to re-equip with the Hunter. In the meantime, the Northrop F-5E was bought to supercede the Hunter in the interceptor role, enabling Fliegerstaffeln 3, 15 and 20, along with 6ieme Escadrille to discard their Venoms and stand up on the Hunter.

Uniquely, a portion of the Swiss Hunter fleet was held in reserve, with the aircraft stowed in special hangers that were tunnelled into the sides of mountains. The aircraft were

J-4015 was given this outlandish 'graffiti' scheme prior to retirement in 1994. She is seen here in company with J-4068
(© Courtesy Swiss Armed Forces)

Château Gruyères provides the spectacular backdrop for J-4119 of Fliegerstaffel 2
(© Courtesy Swiss Armed Forces)

suspended from cables on rails running the length of the ceiling; kept at immediate readiness, they would use specially-prepared sections of public road for take-offs and landings in the unlikely event of war. Swiss Hunters did not see any combat, although one reputedly did score a 'kill' – on another Hunter – in an accident during a live-fire exercise, the aggrieved pilot thankfully ejecting unharmed!

Perhaps the most famous Swiss unit to operate the Hunter was Fliegerstaffel 11, which was responsible for operating the 'Patrouille Suisse' aerobatic team. The team formed in 1964 as a 4-ship unit to celebrate EXPO 1964 in Lausanne and for the 50th anniversary of the Swiss Air force; this was enlarged to 5 aircraft in 1970 and to 6 Hunters in 1978. Until 1978, the team only performed in Switzerland due to the country's strict neutrality;

the team's first foreign performance was at Salon-de-Provence in France. Their shows abroad brought many accolades including trophies at the prestigious International Air Tattoo in Britain. Up until 1989, the unit's Hunters retained standard Swiss AF camouflage, but this was then enhanced by the addition of a large Swiss AF roundel on their undersides. The team flew close to 370 accident-free displays in 30 years on the Hunter, ending in 1994 with a switch to the F-5E.

Switzerland's Hunters gained enhancements throughout their career, starting with a 1963 decision to equip 50 aircraft with wiring and pylons to operate the AIM-9B Sidewinder missile; all subsequent aircraft delivered had this capability built-in. From 1974, the single-seaters were fitted with the SAAB BT-9K bombsight. 12 were converted for use as target tugs and were

Switzerland is one of a handful of countries that uses its road network as auxiliary runways. J-4056 is seen on the N8 autobahn near Alpnach
(© Courtesy Swiss Armed Forces)

fitted with a locally-built towing/winching unit that was carried on an inboard stores pylon. Some sources claim that the T.68s were fitted with bombsights and were even wired for Sidewinders.

Under the ambitious 'Hunter 80' programme, the Hunter's ground-attack abilities were enhanced by the provision for carriage of BL755 Cluster Bomb Units (CBUs) and, in at least 40 aircraft, Maverick Air-to-Ground Missiles (AGMs). They also received AN/ALE-39 chaff/flare dispensers in lengthened link cartridge collector pods, and US-built AN/APR-9 radar warning receivers (RWR) in the nose and on the tailplane bullet.

The T.68s were not only used for conversion training, but also for the electronic countermeasures (ECM) role, carrying a locally-built T-708 ECM pod on an outboard pylon that contained an RF jammer in the front and a AN/ALE-39 chaff/flare dispenser in the rear, the right-seater controlling the ECM gear.

At their height, Hunters equipped a total of nine squadrons, but with the end of the Cold War, aircraft were retired and units disbanded. The final 5 squadrons gave up their aircraft in 1994,

ending 35 years in service. Of the 160 Hunters in Swiss service, 26 were lost in accidents; sadly, 15 aircrew were lost.

Under Swiss law, military goods and weapons are prohibited from sale abroad, so the original plan was to scrap all the Hunters in situ; however, it was discovered that a loophole in the law allowed the aircraft to be given away. Therefore, for a nominal repositioning fee, many Hunters ended up in museums and flying collections around the globe, and today, many of the world's airworthy Hunters are these former Swiss Air Force aircraft, including those operated in a semi-military role by Hawker Hunter Aviation and Northern Lights. Many more fly on the airshow circuit, a reminder of the grace and presence of this classic jet aircraft.

Precision formation work was always a hallmark of the Patrouille Suisse; the unit, formally known as Fliegerstaffel 11, used the Hunter from 1964 to 1994
(© Courtesy Swiss Armed Forces)

Singaporean AF 533, seen here prior to delivery in 1993, is one of around 30 airframes that survive in Australia
(© Courtesy RSAF)

The Hunter
in Action

Given its longevity and overall good performance, it should come as no surprise that the Hunter saw active combat with almost half of the air forces it saw service with. From Suez in 1956 to Lebanon in the mid-1980s and beyond, the Hunter proved to be a sterling workhorse.

Here is a brief summary of the Hunter's combat record, in alphabetic order:

RAF Combat Service

During the Suez Crisis of 1956, Hunter F.5s of No. 1 and No. 34 Squadrons (The Tangmere Wing) were based at RAF Akrotiri in Cyprus as part of Operation Musketeer. They were initially engaged in flying escort missions for English Electric Canberra bombers tasked with bombing missions into Egypt; however, once it was apparent that the Egyptian Air Force was not a serious threat in intercepting the Canberras, the Hunters were put on local air defence against possible retaliatory attacks by Egyptian Air Force Ilyushin Il-28 bombers. Once these had been put out of action, the Tangmere Wing was freed up for fighter sweeps. No Hunter experienced air-to-air combat during these operations. A handful of Hunter F.4s from 111 Squadron was also on hand at Malta to provide air defence.

The Hunter FGA.9 was specifically designed for use by the RAF's Middle East Air Force (MEAF), replacing the de Havilland Venom. It entered service with No. 8 Sqn at Khormaksar in Aden in 1960, followed shortly thereafter by 208 Sqn at Eastleigh in Kenya. 8 Sqn was in action shortly after, as in the summer of 1961, Iraq was making threatening noises regarding newly-independent Kuwait. Bound by treaty obligations, Britain dispatched both 8 and 208 to Kuwait, along with some Shackletons and Canberras, followed by two Royal Navy carriers. In addition, Nos. 43 and 54 Sqns deployed from Britain to Cyprus. The Iraqis backed down, though they would change their minds in a few decades, and the Hunters were withdrawn,

though both 8 and 208 were now based at Khormaksar, with one forward stationed at Bahrain as a deterrent.

The Hunters stationed in Aden did see combat shortly afterwards. A socialist-inspired insurgency flared up in Aden, with the Aden Protectorate, part of the British-inspired South Arabian Federation, in 1962, supported by the new military government in Yemen and Egyptian President Abdel Gamal Nasser, a strong anti-colonialist. The new Front for the Liberation of South Yemen, or FLOSY, began a campaign of urban terrorism and support for back country tribesmen. The Hunters, in conjunction with RAF Shackletons, dropped warning leaflets and bombed recalcitrant villages (following fair warning given by leaflet drops) and insurgent installations in operations reminiscent of the Air Policing strategy used in Iraq and Afghanistan in the 1930s. Furthermore, they provided air cover for Special Air Service (SAS) commandos on raids into insurgent territories such as the Radfan region. Weapons used included 20- and 1,000-lb bombs, 3-in rockets and, of course, the four 30mm cannon.

Further support was added in 1963, when 43 Sqn deployed from Britain, meaning that two squadrons were now permanently based in Aden, with the third in Bahrain. Both squadrons were now also providing combat air patrols, as the Yemani Air Force began crossing the border on bombing raids against border villages. The deterrent value of these Hunters ended this swiftly.

In 1967, the new British Labour government announced the withdrawal from Aden and independence for the South Arabian Federation, and Hunters provided top cover for the evacuation of British subjects and troops, 8 Sqn moving to Bahrain and 43 Sqn disbanding at Khormaksar. It was originally intended to leave behind four Hunters to form a new South Arabian Air Force, but when it became clear that the hoped-for friendly regime was not going to materialize, the aircraft were evacuated

India's Hunters saw service in two major wars, and acquitted themselves well, especially in the ground attack role
(© Jack Cook, via Srecko Bradic)

to Bahrain with the rest.

The Hunter FGA.9 was a natural to replace the Venom with the Far East Air Force (FEAF) in addition to the MEAF, the type deploying with 20 and 28 Sqns, based at Tengah, Singapore and Kai Tak, Hong Kong respectively.

In the post-colonial period of South East Asian history, the long-running 'confrontation' with Indonesia over the status of various Malay provinces was not as hot as some, but nevertheless, it did run very warm for long periods. The RAF's Hunters were amongst the most advanced aircraft in the area at the time and provided much-needed support for hard-pressed and thinly-spread ground forces over the vastness of the disputed region.

The first manifestation of Indonesian interference was during the 1962 Brunei Revolt, when rebels backed by the Sukarno Government in Jakarta took European hostages, with the aim of preventing the Kingdom, along with Sarawak and Sabah, from joining the Federation of Malaysia. Four 20 Sqn Hunters flew from Tengah and staged mock attacks on the building where the hostages were being held, firing their cannon into the jungle as an additional inducement. The hostages were released, and the revolt failed.

Indonesian tactics changed to infiltrations along the long and thinly-guarded borders of Sarawak and Sabah, where Indonesian-supported guerillas would cross in numbers to harass villages and plantations. Some incursions by Indonesian special forces troops were made using C-130 transports. British forces, including the Gurkhas and the SAS, were deployed to counter these incursions, often aided by RAF Hunters which flew air support strikes on enemy troop concentrations using rockets and cannon.

The British government also made it clear that aerial intruders would be engaged. While C-130 flights were confined to the cover of darkness, occasional incursions by Indonesian Air Force MiG fighters were made. It is said that on one occasion a Hunter of 20 Sqn got into a manoeuvering match with a MiG, which ended with the MiG pilot losing control of his aircraft and crashing into terrain. If true, this would be the only instance of an RAF Hunter scoring an aerial victory.

The 'Confrontation' gradually fizzled out as it became clear that the Malay people and the British government would not back down, and abated in 1966 when Sukarno was ousted in a coup.

Chile

Chilean Air Force Hunters played a small but important role in

the September 1973 military coup that ousted the Marxist President Allende. Hunters of Grupo 7 bombed and strafed the presidential palace, Allende's home, and government-run radio stations in the capital Santiago.

While not actively engaged, Hunters were kept on alert during the 1982 Falklands War between Britain and Argentina; historical antagonisms and long-running border disputes having long plagued the area. Interestingly, Britain supplied more Hunters to Chile after the war in recognition of 'services rendered.'

India

Perhaps the most extensive combat career for the Hunter was in the hands of the Indian Air Force. As one of the earliest and most extensive Hunter users, this is not a surprise. The first use of the Hunter in action was during the 1961 Indian invasion of Goa, then a Portuguese possession. Indian intelligence suggested that a squadron of F-86 Sabres was stationed at a military airfield in Goa, although this proved not to be the case. Nevertheless, Hunters performed Combat Air Patrols (CAP) over Portuguese airfields for the first few days of the invasion, whilst others flew interdiction missions, including attacks on the main radio station. No Hunters were shot down or damaged by enemy action during the war.

The next conflict involving India was very much larger and with considerable air combat; this was the 1965 Indo-Pakistan War, or the Second Kashmir War as it was centred on that hotly-disputed region. During the 1965 War, Indian Hunters served with four squadrons; 7 and 27 at Halwara, close to the Kashmir region, and 17 and 20 Squadrons based at Poona. Besides their involvement in the air war, Hunters were also heavily involved in close support and ground attack, destroying many Pakistani tanks and vehicles, as well as attacking infrastructure well behind the frontline – Sarghoda airfield being one example, as mentioned below – including the railways and power stations.

While it is not the place of this book to sort through the various contradictory claims related to the cause and results of the war, it is sufficient to say that Indian Hunters were heavily involved in both air-to-air and air-to-ground combat. Independent sources attribute 8 air combat 'kills' to Hunters, mostly F-86 Sabres, while 9 were lost, all to Pakistani F-86s. The famous 'Battle of Sarghoda' airfield, where one Pakistani pilot is claimed to have shot down 5 Hunters in a couple of minutes, is probably exaggerated – India admits to only three Hunters being lost over the course of 4 raids on the airfield that day. Nevertheless, it appears that the Hunter and Sabre were evenly

Hunters 803 and 810 of 2 Squadron Royal Jordanian Air Force, fly over their homeland. It is likely that both were destroyed in the 1967 fighting
(© courtesy John Adams Collection)

matched in the hands of their Indian and Pakistani pilots.

After 5 weeks of bitter fighting in which neither side gained a decisive edge, an uneasy ceasefire was agreed that remained in place until 1971. However, conflict was never far from the surface in the region, and war erupted again following Indian involvement in East Pakistan, now known as Bangladesh, during the Pakistan Civil War. Pakistan launched a pre-emptive strike on Indian Air Force bases, followed by large scale armoured attacks. India responded on both land and air, Hunters being heavily involved in halting Pakistani advances through the destruction of tanks and transports, while they were also used in attacks on strategic targets deep inside Pakistan, including oil refineries, dams and power stations. In the air, it was quickly found that the Hunter was inferior to the Pakistani Air Force's MiGs and Mirages, approximately 12 being lost in air-to-air combat, while another 5 were lost on ground-attack missions. Two victories were claimed by Hunters, but in this war, it was far more useful in the ground-attack role, playing a large part in halting the advance of at least one Pakistani armoured division.

Following the war, the Indian Air Force was rapidly built up, with obsolescent aircraft such as the Hunter being replaced by modern MiG-21s and -23s, and Jaguars.

Iraq

Iraqi Hunters saw action in both the 1967 Six-Day War and the Yom Kippur War in 1973, serving in both air combat and ground-support roles. In the air-to-air role, there are conflicting claims for aircraft downed on both the Iraqi and Israeli sides; the Israelis claimed 16 Iraqi Hunters shot down, though it is likely that it will never be known for sure who did what. It is known that Jordanian pilots, their Hunters having been destroyed on the ground by the Israelis, were seconded to the Iraqi Air Force for the remainder of the War and did fly Iraqi Hunters; other foreign pilots flew Iraqi Hunters during both conflicts as well, including Saudis and at least one Pakistani.

Iraqi Hunters were phased out of service during the 1970s in favour of the Sukhoi Su-7, but they were still active in the operational training role into the 1980s and it is strongly rumoured that they were used to spray nerve gas on Kurdish villages in the north of Iraq, and possibly also against Iranian troops in the long-running Iran-Iraq War.

During the 1991 Gulf War, the remaining airframes were used as decoys on various Iraqi airfields; at least one was the subject of a guided-bomb attack captured on film by the US Air Force. Given subsequent events, it seems unlikely that any Hunters have survived in Iraq.

Jordan

With disputes over water rights running high, the mid-sixties were a tense time in the valley of the River Jordan. There were frequent border clashes as each side tried to prevent infrastructure work, and air support was used on occasion. This led to direct air-to-air clashes over the area. The best known of these was what the Jordanians refer to as the Battle of the Dead Sea in December 1964, when Royal Jordanian Air Force (RJAF) Hunters clashed with Israeli Mirage IIIs, claiming one plus three more damaged, for no losses. The Israelis admit to the loss, through fuel starvation.

Another similar incident occurred in November 1966 when the Israelis launched a reprisal raid on a border village in the Hebron Mountains of the West Bank. Two pairs of Hunters took off from the King Hussein Air Base at Mafraq and engaged with the Israeli Mirages. One of the Hunters was shot down by an Israeli Mirage III; the pilot managed to eject but did not survive. There were two Jordanian claims from the battle and it was later confirmed that one Israeli Mirage III landed damaged and the

other, also damaged, crashed short of the runway.

During the June 1967 Six-Day War, the Israelis feared a joint Arab invasion and launched a pre-emptive strike on Egyptian airbases on June 5th. In response to this, small numbers of RJAF Hunters dropped bombs on Israeli airfields; an Israeli transport was claimed destroyed on the ground. Shortly after, the Israeli Air Force turned its attention eastwards and launched a massive attack against RJAF bases; RJAF pilots engaged the attacking Israeli aircraft, claiming three. During these attacks, the Israelis destroyed around 20 Hunters on the ground and two more in the air; both Mafraq, the main Hunter base, and Amman airfields were put out of action. This effectively removed the RJAF from further participation in the war, though, as mentioned above, Jordanian pilots thereafter flew Iraqi Hunters until the conclusion of the war. During this period, Jordanian pilots claimed to have shot down three Israeli Mirages and two Vautour bombers heading to attack the Iraqi air base of H3, for the loss of one aircraft; Israel states it lost only two aircraft and downed three Hunters, but has admitted that the mission was aborted. The Hunter force was re-equipped from 1968.

Following the loss of the West Bank territory during the 1967 War, Jordan was faced by a surge in popularity of the Palestinian movement amongst the thousands of refugees living in camps on the eastern shores of the Jordan River; this threatened to de-stabilize Jordan, which was, and still is a constitutional monarchy. Many factions of the Palestinian Liberation Organisation (PLO) were active in their opposition to the King, and King Hussein ordered the army to target these rebels. On September 6 the PFLP (Popular Front for the Liberation of Palestine) hijacked British, Swiss and US airliners, forcing them to land at Dawson's Field in Jordan; the hostages were released at the end of September, but the airliners were spectacularly blown up.

Martial law was declared on September 15 and on the 20th, Syrian armoured forces, supported by Palestinian guerillas, crossed the border and engaged the Jordanian army. This armoured column, aimed at the capital Amman, was targeted by waves of attacks by RJAF Hunters with anti-tank rockets and cannon fire, to such devastating effect that the Syrians' momentum was halted. By the afternoon of the 22nd the Syrians had retreated back across the border. One Hunter was lost; the pilot parachuted to safety but was taken prisoner by the Syrians, but was later released.

With Jordan effectively on the sidelines during the Syrian-Egyptian offensive during the 1973 Yom Kippur War, the RJAF Hunter fleet stood by in a defensive posture and saw no reported combat during that war. Retired shortly afterwards, the remaining aircraft were gifted to the Sultan of Oman.

Lebanon

Hunters were ordered for the Lebanese Air Force following the 1958 crisis that threatened civil war between the Christian Maronites and Muslims, and the subsequent US intervention; indeed, US offshore funding was used for this purchase and others to bolster the Lebanese military.

The 1967 Six-Day War embroiled the region; however, Lebanon did not officially take part due in part to the large and influential Christian population who did not share the Arab world's position regarding Israel. Despite this, the first day of the war did see Israeli Air Force Mirages cross the border during their attacks on neighbouring Syria. Hunters were scrambled in response to this and one was shot down, the pilot surviving.

However, from 1968, the neutral course adopted by the Lebanese government was eroded by building ethnic tensions and by the presence of the Palestinian Liberation Organisation (PLO) in southern Lebanon, where it gradually built enough strength to create an effective 'guerilla state' as a base to attack

Israel. The erosion of central power led to factional fighting between rival militias that a severely weakened Christian government was virtually powerless to prevent. The air force still operated at the behest of the government but was really a shadow force, unable to bring effective power to bear. Hunters were used sporadically, a number being lost on ground support missions.

Following the 1982 Israeli invasion of southern Lebanon in a successful effort to expel the PLO, the remnants of the Lebanese Air Force played a more active role than previously. During fierce fighting in the capital, Beirut, Hunters could regularly be seen overhead. However, the virtual collapse of the armed forces in 1984, and the withdrawal of foreign troops who had supported a fragile pro-western government, led to the grounding of the Hunters and other air force assets.

In 2007, the Lebanese armed forces began a period of quiet expansion following a period of relative stability. One of the aims of this expansion has been the creation of effective ground support forces; to this end, some Hunters have been pulled out of mothballs and restored to flying condition. While it is to be hoped that they do not need to see active combat, it is encouraging that the Hunter is still considered worthy of a return to useful service.

Oman

The Sultan of Oman's Air Force (SOAF) was formed in 1959, and acquired Hunters in the early 1970s to help combat incursions by Yemeni guerillas and Omani insurgent groups. Attacks, using rockets and cannon, were often made against guerilla camps in Yemeni territory, leading to the loss of at least one Hunter, and damage to others. It appears that the aircraft were flown by (mostly ex-RAF) mercenaries.

Peru

Despite certain reports to the contrary, it appears that all Peruvian Hunters had been withdrawn from service prior to the 1981 'Paquisha' War between Peru and Equador over long-standing border disputes.

Rhodesia/Zimbabwe

The Rhodesians used their Hunter FGA.9s extensively against ZANU and ZAPU guerillas in the late 1960s and throughout the 1970s, including cross-border strikes against terrorist camps placed in neighbouring countries across the south African region.

Shortly after delivery of its Hunters, Rhodesia announced its Unilateral Declaration of Independence (UDI), and the aircraft were involved in patrolling the border with Zambia, where the British had stationed some RAF Javelins as a token deterrence. Britain had placed an embargo on spares and servicing, and it was only due to the ingenuity of the Rhodesian Air Force technicians, and some covert help from fellow pariah state South Africa, that kept the aircraft flying. Many local modifications were fitted, including napalm, cluster bombs (often filled with flechettes – metal darts), fragmentation bombs (known as the Golf bomb) and other anti-personnel weaponry, and a few were wired for AAMs by the South Africans in the early 1970s – these being either Sidewinders or the South African Darter missile. At least one aircraft was equipped with a drop tank fitted with cameras for use as a reconnaissance pod. These modifications were all the more necessary when, in 1972, the fledgling black guerilla movement started to flex its muscles and began its long and brutal struggle for majority rule.

The Hunter fleet bore the brunt of the fighting, alongside a handful of Canberra and Vampires, and were involved in many operations against guerilla camps across southern Africa, the widespread use of anti-personnel weapon causing massive casualties amongst the guerilla forces. Despite this, the government was forced to concede that they could not win the bitter war and so white minority rule was ended in 1980 and Rhodesia became Zimbabwe.

It has been reported that Zimbabwean Hunters were used to support Laurent Kabila during the 1998 Congo War, but it is much more likely that the aircraft involved were BAe Hawks.

Somalia

The regime of Marxist Somali President Siad Barre used Hunters for indiscriminate bombings on his own population during the civil war in the late 1980s. These were based at Berbera, an important deep-ocean port in north-west Somalia, and were flown and maintained by mercenaries, mostly from Zimbabwe and South Africa. The Hunters were also flown operationally against anti-government groups based in Ethiopia and remote areas of Somalia. Following the ousting of Barre, the air force disintegrated and the Hunters were left to rot.

Hunter Camouflage and Markings

British military aircraft, the Hunter included of course, are painted according to Ministry of Defence guidelines in accordance with British Standards Institute specifications. The main specification that concerns the Hunter is BS381C, which was first issued in 1930 and regularly revised and updated since. All colours quoted below include their BS381C number, e.g. Dark Green 641.

Throughout the Hunter's service career, the Ministry promulgated changes to aircraft camouflage and markings; while these were issued on a certain date, operational and other requirements meant that it could be some months before all aircraft colours or markings were repainted to conform to the new patterns, therefore anomalies are frequent.

Export aircraft that left Hawkers' factories were all painted to the same pattern as their RAF counterparts; however, the colours used varied from country to country, though most fell into two groups – temperate finish – the same as the RAF; or desert finish, most frequently seen on Middle Eastern customers' aircraft. There were exceptions and these will be dealt with separately. Operating countries frequently repainted their aircraft in a different scheme.

Hawkers used rubber masking mats to spray new-build aircraft, so the camouflage demarcation lines were hard-edged. It is said that they also had a man at the end of the production line, whose sole job was to remove any over- or under-spray with car polish! Rebuilt airframes, and aircraft emerging from RAF depots often exhibited soft-edged camouflage – and some aircraft exhibited both hard- and soft-edged camouflage at the same time. Close study of photos is recommended for individual airframes.

RAF

Fighters and Ground Attack – F.1–6, FGA.9 and FR.10

At the time the Hunter started to leave the production line, RAF fighters were painted in an overall Aluminium scheme as promulgated in 1945; however, only a handful of Hunters received this finish, as a new Air Ministry Order (AMO) was issued in April 1951, heralding the return of camouflage to RAF aircraft. Between this time and 1966, RAF Hunters were given a disruptive camouflage pattern of Dark Green 641 and Dark Sea Grey 638, with Aluminium (officially known at that time as High Speed Silver) undersides. There was no wraparound on the wing leading edges at this time. Finish was high gloss and aircraft were painted using a standard diagram that demarcated the disruptive scheme for the upper surfaces. Until the FGA.9, factory-finished aircraft appear to have all had sharp-edged colour demarcations, but rebuilt, repainted and depot-serviced aircraft often appear with feather-edged camouflage – this being particularly applicable to the FGA.9 and to export aircraft.

Until late 1954, aircraft left the production line with a high gloss finish cellulose paint to DTD 900, but a change in specifications to DTD 899 led to an eggshell or satin finish. Broadly, this occurred quite early in F.4 and 5 production and most appear to have had this finish. Around 1961, the specification was changed again, as the cellulose paints were subject to weathering. Weathering-resistant epoxy paints to DTD 5555 were now to be used. Finally, in 1969, DTD 5580 polyurethane paints were specified, these giving either gloss or matt finish depending on the circumstances – most Hunters now appear to have been matt finished.

Starting in 1966, the undersides were repainted in Light Aircraft Grey 627, and the wraparound leading edge was introduced. From 1970, the overall finish was changed from satin to matt. Very late in the Hunter's career, some F.6/FGA.9 aircraft introduced a wraparound camouflage finish, eliminating the LAG undersides.

With regards to the national markings carried by Hunters, the roundels were what is known at Type D, and painted in Post Office Red 538, White and Roundel Blue 110. For the upper wing surfaces, these were specified as 48in, while lower wing and rear fuselage were to 36in. The red was to be 1/3rd of the diameter of the roundel, and white to 2/3rds. The fin marking was 18in wide and 21.5in high, divided equally into thirds with the red portion closest to the fin leading edge.

After around 1970, new toned-down markings were introduced that eliminated the white portions of the roundels and fin flashes. While the overall dimensions remained the same, the red portion now occupied half of the roundels and flash.

Aircraft identity numbers, or serials, were set at 8in for the rear fuselage; these were generally in Night (black), but could often be found in White on later marks. Underwing serial presentation was generally also in Night and was 24in high. On the F.1 and 2, they were presented as a single angled row, but for later marks where drop tanks could be carried, the presentation was changed to two rows perpendicular to the centerline. In both cases, the serials were presented so that they could be read from the rear on the starboard wing and from the front on the port wing.

Unit markings could take many forms, but the most common with the Hunter were nose markings and bars to each side of the rear fuselage roundel. The term 'emblem' is properly used for the officially approved design unique to a squadron, which is in turn the centerpiece of the squadron's 'badge,' the design of which is approved by the Royal College of Arms and granted by the reigning monarch. As the Hunter entered service in the reign of Queen Elizabeth II, the badge is surmounted by the Queen's Crown. The squadron badge or emblem was often displayed on the nose, frequently flanked by the squadron's unique bars.

Trainers – T.7

From service entry in 1958 until 1966, RAF trainers, including the Hunters serving with front-line squadrons,

No.1 Squadron FGA.9
FGA.9 of No.1 Squadron while part of the strike component, along with 54 Squadron, of Transport Command's No.38 Group. c1962

4 Squadron F.6
F.6 of No. 4 Squadron, 122 Wing, 2 Group, 2TAF at RAF Jever, Germany c1960. 4 Squadron was the longest serving Hunter squadron in the RAF, first receiving F.4s in July 1955 and switching to the Mk 6 in February 1957. The squadron was disbanded on 30 December 1960 only to reform the following day when 79 Squadron was renumbered '4' and had its Swift FR.5s replaced with Hunter FR.10s. With the advent of the F.6 the large rear fuselage bars were reduced in size and moved to the nose to surround the 'sunburst' and pierced '4' design. Later, a small Union flag was applied to each side of the nose

No.26 Squadron F.4
F.4 of Flying Officer Nigel Walpole, 26 Squadron, 124 Wing, 2 Group, 2TAF based at RAF Oldenburg, Germany. c1956. Several variations in design of the Springbok's head in the squadron flash were seen, but the head always faced forward on the port side of the nose, and aft on the starboard

No.28 Squadron FGA.9
FGA.9 of Hong Kong-based 28 Squadron after re-equipping with the Mk 9 in July 1962

No.45 Squadron FGA.9
FGA.9 of 45 Squadron at RAF West Raynham, August 1972. The following month 45 Squadron moved to RAF Wittering in company with 58 Squadron

No.54 Squadron F.6
F.6 of 54 Squadron, RAF Stradishall, 1957. Note the later style of squadron flash with fewer and larger checks and white disc behind the lion

No.56 Squadron F.6
F.6 of 56 Squadron. The squadron received the Mk 6 in November 1958 and operated it until re-equipped with Lightnings in January 1961

Colour Art © Mark Gauntlett

No.58 Squadron FGA.9
FGA.9 of 58 Squadron at RAF Wittering, the squadron's base for the entirity of its period as a Hunter unit. c1974

No.65 Squadron F.6
F.6 of 65 Squadron which, in company with 64 Squadron operating Javelins, flew the Mk 6 from RAF Duxford between December 1956 and March 1961

No.71 Squadron F.4
F.4 of 71 Squadron, the badge of which reflects the squadron's history as the first American-manned 'Eagle' squadron in 1940. 71 operated the Mk 4 as part of 135 Wing, 83 Group, 2TAF at RAF Bruggen for only 13 months before being disbanded in May 1957. Squadron markings were reduced in size and moved to the nose, from the rear fuselage, just prior to disbandment

No.93 Squadron F.6
F.6 of Flt Lt Mick Ryan, 93 Squadron, 122 Wing, 2 Group, 2TAF at RAF Jever, Germany. 93 Squadron replaced its F.4s in March 1957 and subsequently operated the F.6 until disbandment in December 1960. With the change to the F.6 came the repositioning of the squadron markings from the fuselage to the nose. This initally only included the 'escarbuncle' design, but later the bars with arrowhead design followed by the Union flag were added

No.130 Squadron F.4
F.4 of 130 Squadron, 135 Wing, 83 Group, 2TAF based at RAF Bruggen, Germany. A short-lived squadron, 130 operated the F.4 between March 1956 and disbandment in May 1957. The elephant's head in the squadron flash, adapted from the squadron badge, became more detailed as time went on but always faced forward on the port side of the nose, and aft on the starboard

No.234 Squadron F.4
F.4 of 234 Squadron C.O. Sqn Ldr Ted Riseley at RAF Geilenkirchen, Germany just prior to the squadron's disbandment in July 1957. 234 was one of two Hunter squadrons based at Geilenkirchen, the other being No. 3 Squadron, and received its first F.4s in April 1956. The griffon, derived from the squadron badge, faced forward on both sides of the aircraft

No.263 Squadron F.2
F.2 of 263 Squadron who operated the Mk 2 alongside the similarly marked and Sapphire-powered F.5 for most of its time as a Hunter unit at RAF Wattisham

Colour Art © Mark Gauntlett

wore an overall gloss Aluminium (High Speed Silver) finish. Until 1961, they wore gloss Golden Yellow 356, or Lemon 355 bands around the rear fuselage and chord-wise around each wing. This was changed in 1961 to dayglo (red or orange-red) areas or stripes, particularly on the fin, wingtips and/or nose.

In 1966, the basic airframe colour was changed to gloss Light Aircraft Grey 627, while operational squadrons were now permitted to camouflage their trainers in the same manner as their primary aircraft.

Aircraft at Flying Training Schools received a new colour scheme in 1970, this consisting of White with areas of gloss Signal Red 537 and Light Aircraft Grey 627.

Royal Navy

GA.11, PR.11

As introduced in 1961, single-seat FAA Hunters carried a scheme of gloss Extra Dark Sea Grey 640 over White. From 1984, and especially in FRADU service, the aircraft were repainted in overall gloss Dark Sea Grey 638.

T.8

Like their RAF counterparts, RN T.8s initially wore an overall Aluminium finish with Yellow trainer bands, but from 1962, the Yellow bands gave way to large areas of Dayglo Red-Orange on the wings, tailplanes, fin and nose. From 1969, the basic airframe colour was changed to Light Aircraft Grey 627. Those aircraft in service after 1984 with FRADU were painted overall Dark Sea Grey 638, while the T.8Ms used for training Sea Harrier pilots were painted in the Extra Dark Sea Grey 640 over White scheme at first, before also switching to the overall Dark Sea Grey scheme.

Exports

Aircraft built by the Dutch and Belgians were finished in standard RAF colours, as were export machines made by Hawkers for Chile, Denmark, India, Iraq, Jordan, Kenya, Lebanon, Peru, Rhodesia, and Switzerland. Sweden was unique in specifying Dark Green single-colour upper surfaces, with light grey/blue undersides.

Chile, Denmark, Oman, and Rhodesia/Zimbabwe later repainted their aircraft in different schemes as their individual conditions dictated. Chile used a two-tone grey wraparound scheme on their Hunter 80 aircraft; an experimental desert-type scheme was applied to a handful of aircraft. Late in their life, Denmark's Hunters were painted in an overall dark olive green colour which faded badly in service, while Rhodesia/Zimbabwe used an overall Dark Earth colour, with a disruptive Dark Green pattern. Singapore adopted a three-tone upper scheme similar to the USAF's South East Asia pattern.

Those aircraft delivered by Hawkers to some Middle Eastern nations were given a desert scheme of the following colours manufactured by ICI:
- Brown – ICI F407-1815
- Sand – ICI F407-1814
- Deep Sky Blue – ICI F407-1813

Discussions with ICI indicated that these colours were discontinued many years ago, and they could not supply any details of these colours, or whether there are any alternatives in the BS, FS, RAL etc. systems. However, BS381C:350 Dark Earth appears to be a close match for the ICI Brown, and PRU Blue is close to the Deep Sky Blue. Mark Gauntlett, who owns a cockpit section from a Qatari machine, was able to supply the following RGB matches, based on paint from his airframe

that he uncovered during restoration:
- Brown – R:145 G:116 B:59 – a good match for Dark Earth
- Sand – R:205 G:177 B:45 – dark yellow
- Deep Sky Blue – R:68 G:128 B:168 – similar to PRU Blue

It should be noted that the Sand is a strong deep yellow, rather than a sandy colour that the name might imply – comparisons to RAF Light Stone are not appropriate, as that colour is too beige. These colours were used on the Qatari, Abu Dhabi, Kuwaiti and Saudi Hunters and subsequently found their way to the Somali aircraft too as they were passed on by Abu Dhabi.

Colour Side-views* • 1

Hawker P.1067 WB188 – first prototype, mid-1951
Painted in overall 'duck egg green,' similar to RAF Sky. Note the spin parachute housing above the tailcone

Hunter F.1 WT692/S, No 54 Squadron, August 1955
Dark Green and Dark Sea Grey upper surfaces over High Speed Silver undersides. B Flight commander's aircraft with Golden Yellow fin, Roundel Blue flash and Lemon Yellow code letter 'S'. Roundel Blue wingtips. Nosewheel door Golden Yellow with Roundel Blue code.
Scrap view: Squadron emblem – blue rampant lion with red tongue

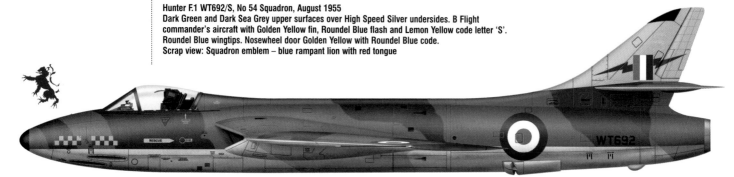

Hunter F.1 WT614/B, Fighter Weapons School, 1956
Dark Green and Dark Sea Grey over High Speed Silver. Code in white with red surround. Code repeated in red on nosewheel door. Note link collector tanks – unusual for an F.1

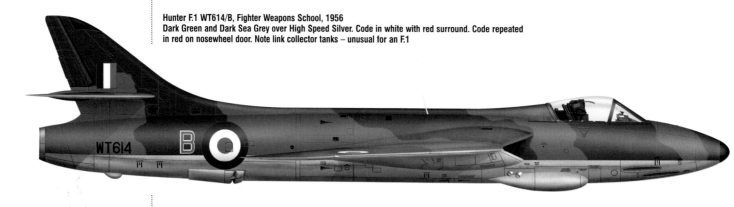

Hunter F.2 WN948/R, No 257 Squadron, 1955
Dark Green and Dark Sea Grey over High Speed Silver. Code in Golden Yellow, squadron bar markings in Bright Green and Golden Yellow – note green is peeling

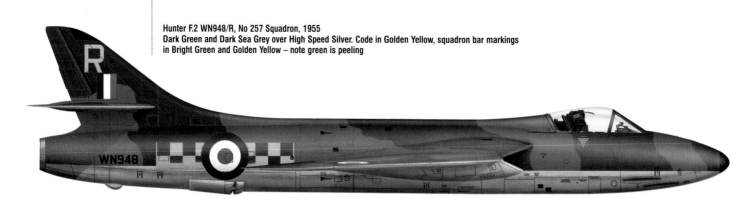

Colour Art © Srecko Bradic   * All these side-views are intended as references for colour and marking purposes and should not be considered as scale plans or technical drawings.

Hunter F.3 WB188, September 1953
Overall gloss Post Office Red 538

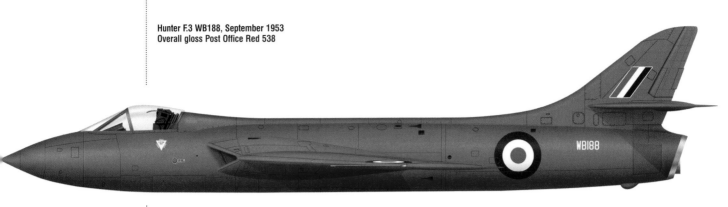

Hunter F.4 WW658/O, No 98 Squadron, 1955
Dark Green and Dark Sea Grey over High Speed Silver. Code letter 'O' in White.
Scrap view shows No 98 Squadron badge in standard frame flanked by markings in Post Office Red and White, as featured on the rear fuselage

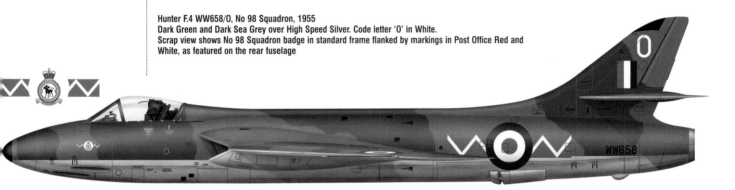

Hunter F.4 XF937/T, No 112 Squadron, 1956
Dark Green and Dark Sea Grey over High Speed Silver. Code letter 'T' in White. Note 'sharkmouth' and eyes on nose in red, white and black. Code letter repeated in red on nosewheel door

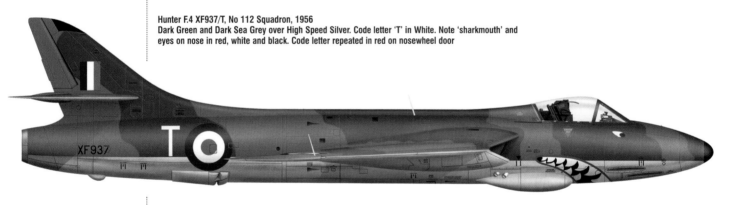

Hunter F.4 WV334/E, No 74 Squadron, 1957
Dark Green and Dark Sea Grey over High Speed Silver. Note 'Exercise Vigilant' special markings – fin painted in white. Code letter 'E' in Golden Yellow, repeated in black on nosewheel door.
Scrap view: No 74 Squadron tiger head marking in black and Golden Yellow

Colour Art © Srecko Bradic

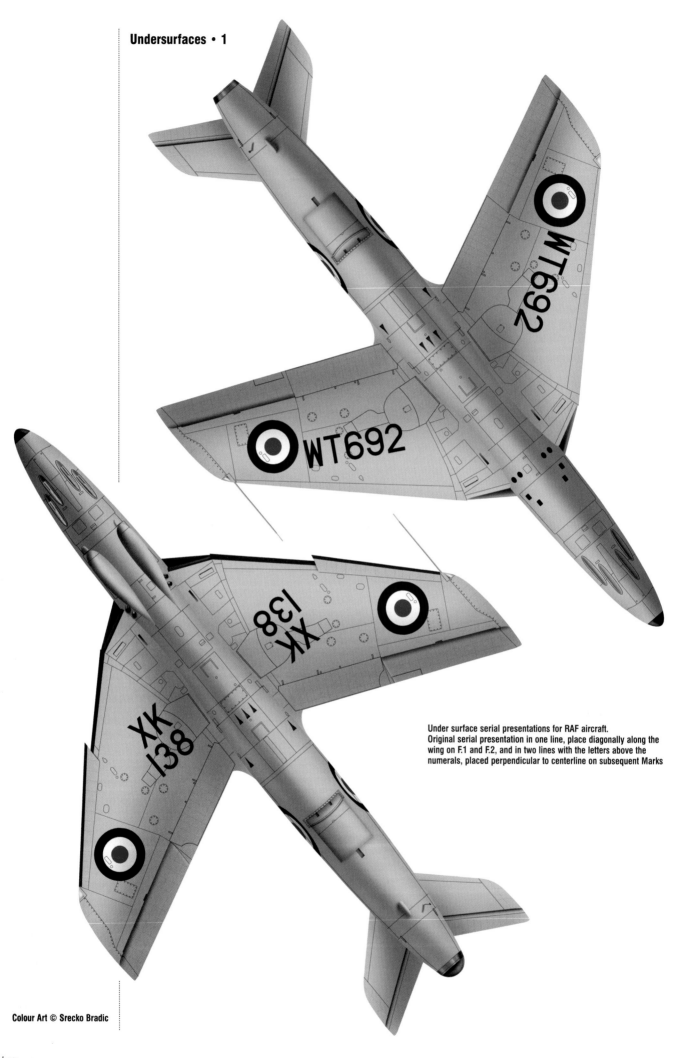

Under surface serial presentations for RAF aircraft.
Original serial presentation in one line, place diagonally along the wing on F.1 and F.2, and in two lines with the letters above the numerals, placed perpendicular to centerline on subsequent Marks

Colour Art © Srecko Bradic

Hunter F.5 WP183/V, No 56 Squadron, 1955
Dark Green and Dark Sea Grey over High Speed Silver. Code letter 'V' in white with red surround, Red and white checked wingtips. Note unusual presentation of the squadron marking on nose, where the usual 'Firebird' emblem has been replaced by a repeat of the code on a light blue disc

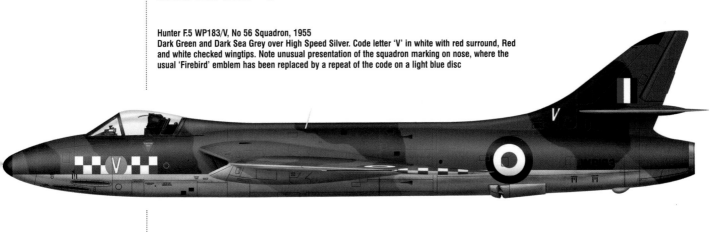

Hunter F.5, WP130/S, No 34 Squadron, Suez Campaign November 1956
Dark Green and Dark Sea Grey over High Speed Silver, with Suez Campaign stripes added. However, this aircraft shows non-standard presentation – the stripes were supposed to be three yellow and two black; local conditions dictated that this a/c had what is thought to be sand-coloured stripes in place of yellow, and the black stripes had yet to be added. Tail code 'S' in yellow with black surround, nose arrowhead emblem in black and yellow with red surround

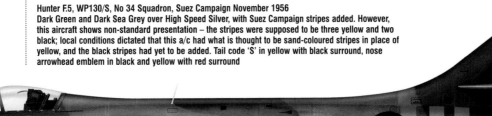

Hunter F.6 XG232/G, No 92 Squadron, 1960
Dark Green and Dark Sea Grey over High Speed Silver. Squadron colours of red and yellow checks on the nose flanking the squadron emblem and under the tailplane. Yellow code letter 'G' on fin. Squadron emblem is a pale green and yellow snake on a red maple leaf – see scrap view. Wingtips were probably yellow

Hunter F.6 XG185/74, No 4 Flying Training School, 1968
Dark Green and Dark Sea Grey over High Speed Silver. White spine, fin, wingtips and drop tanks. Code '74' in large white disc on nose. Unit emblem on fin.
Scrap view – No 4 FTS unit badge in a standard frame

Colour Art © Srecko Bradic

Hunter F.6 XF383, No 216 Squadron, 1980
Wraparound Dark Green and Dark Sea Grey. Note squadron emblem of yellow eagle holding a bombpn the nose, (see scrap view). Hunters were temporary replacement for Buccaneers when the type was grounded after a fatal crash which revealed wing stress problems

Hunter T.7 XL568/X, No 74 Squadron, 1960
Overall High Speed Silver with Golden Yellow trainer bands around wings and rear fuselage. Black code letter 'X' on fin
Scrap view shows No 74 Sqn tiger head and squadron bars on nose

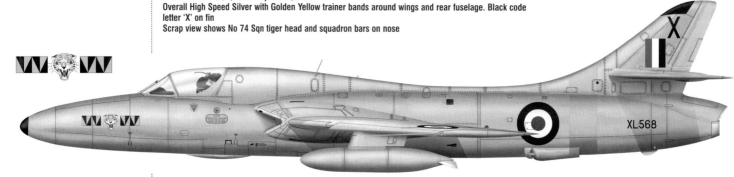

Hunter T.7 XF321/TZ, No 1417 Flight, 1966
Camouflage is very faded Dark Green and Dark Sea Grey over Light Aircraft Grey. This aircraft originally served with the joint No 8/43 Sqn and when it was transferred to 1417 Flt it retained the original squadron markings with the addition of the 1417 pennant on nose – see scrap view. Note white wingtips

Hunter T.7 XL621/81, No 4 Flying Training School, 1973.
Dark Green and Dark Sea Grey over Light Aircraft Grey. White spine, fin and wing outer sections, including the outer pylons. Code '81' in large white disc on nose. Note the red drop tank

Colour Art © Srecko Bradic

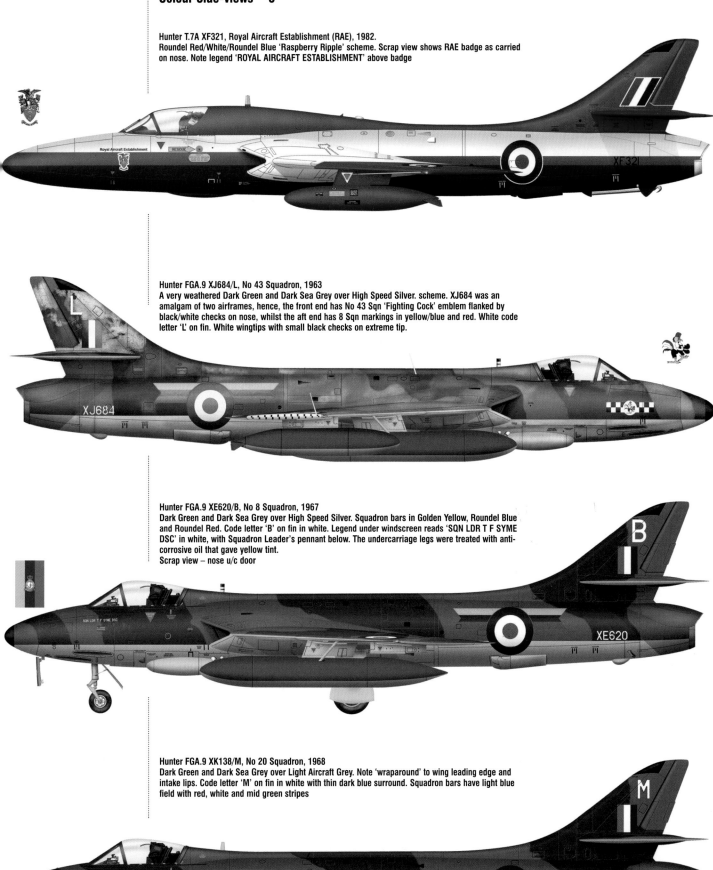

Hunter T.7A XF321, Royal Aircraft Establishment (RAE), 1982.
Roundel Red/White/Roundel Blue 'Raspberry Ripple' scheme. Scrap view shows RAE badge as carried on nose. Note legend 'ROYAL AIRCRAFT ESTABLISHMENT' above badge

Hunter FGA.9 XJ684/L, No 43 Squadron, 1963
A very weathered Dark Green and Dark Sea Grey over High Speed Silver. scheme. XJ684 was an amalgam of two airframes, hence, the front end has No 43 Sqn 'Fighting Cock' emblem flanked by black/white checks on nose, whilst the aft end has 8 Sqn markings in yellow/blue and red. White code letter 'L' on fin. White wingtips with small black checks on extreme tip.

Hunter FGA.9 XE620/B, No 8 Squadron, 1967
Dark Green and Dark Sea Grey over High Speed Silver. Squadron bars in Golden Yellow, Roundel Blue and Roundel Red. Code letter 'B' on fin in white. Legend under windscreen reads 'SQN LDR T F SYME DSC' in white, with Squadron Leader's pennant below. The undercarriage legs were treated with anti-corrosive oil that gave yellow tint.
Scrap view – nose u/c door

Hunter FGA.9 XK138/M, No 20 Squadron, 1968
Dark Green and Dark Sea Grey over Light Aircraft Grey. Note 'wraparound' to wing leading edge and intake lips. Code letter 'M' on fin in white with thin dark blue surround. Squadron bars have light blue field with red, white and mid green stripes

Colour Art © Srecko Bradic

Colour Side-views • 6

Hunter FR.10 WW596/N, No 2 Squadron, 1963
Dark Green and Dark Sea Grey over High Speed Silver. Code letter 'N' in black on white triangle above fin flash.
Scrap view shows No 2 Squadron badge in standard frame

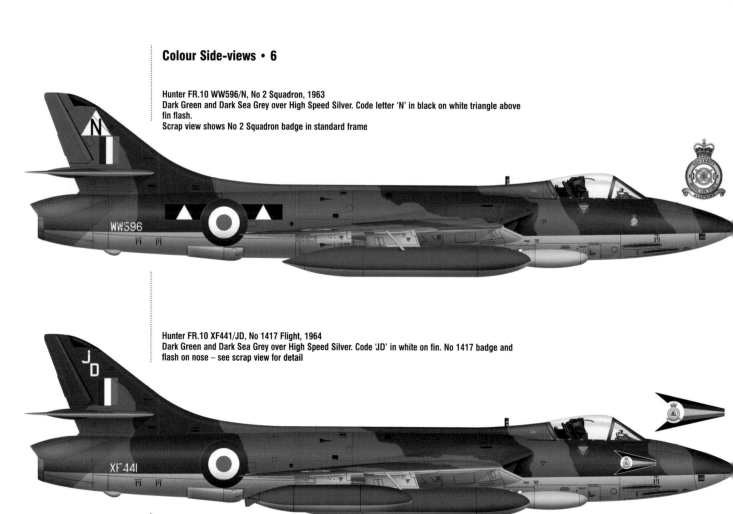

Hunter FR.10 XF441/JD, No 1417 Flight, 1964
Dark Green and Dark Sea Grey over High Speed Silver. Code 'JD' in white on fin. No 1417 badge and flash on nose – see scrap view for detail

Hunter GA.11 XF300/694, No 764 Naval Air Squadron, 1968
Extra Dark Sea Grey over White. Note spine and front of fin in white. Squadron emblem on nose with white and green checks. Letters 'LM' on fin is the base designation code for Lossiemouth.

Below: Upper surface view of Hunter GA.11 XF300/694, No 764 Naval Air Squadron, 1968

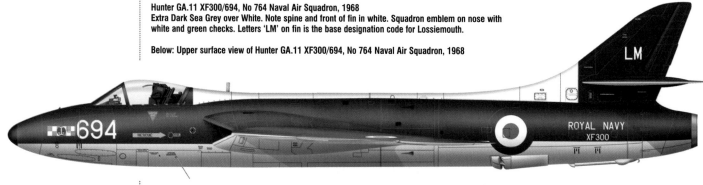

Colour Art © Srecko Bradic

Colour Side-views • 7

Hunter GA.11 XE707/865, FRADU 1985
Overall Dark Sea Grey. Note Harley light in nose. Code 'VL' in black on fin is base designation code for Yeovilton

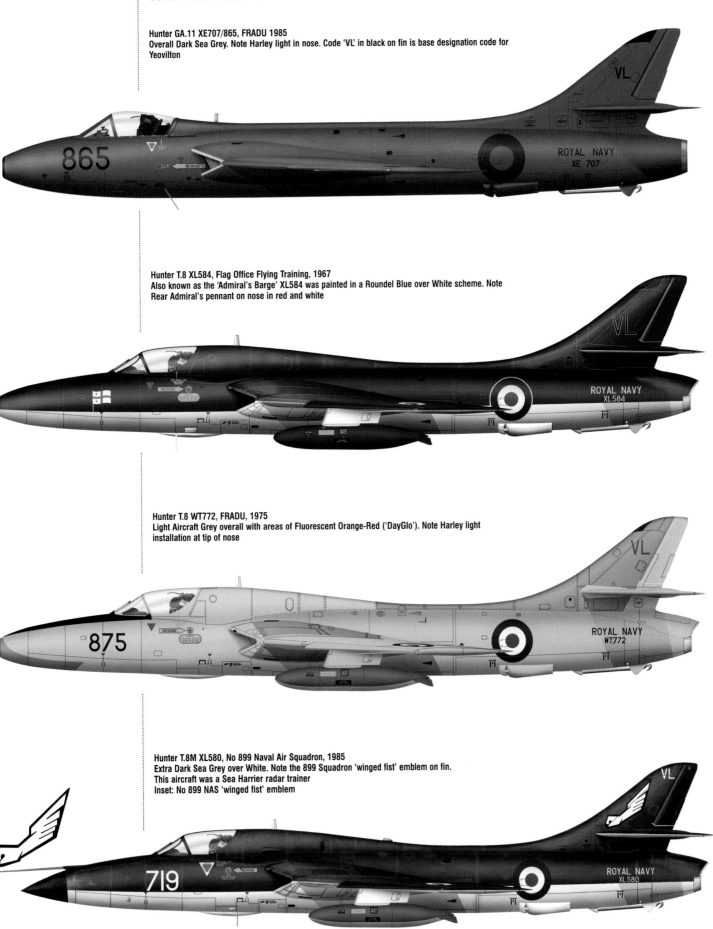

Hunter T.8 XL584, Flag Office Flying Training, 1967
Also known as the 'Admiral's Barge' XL584 was painted in a Roundel Blue over White scheme. Note Rear Admiral's pennant on nose in red and white

Hunter T.8 WT772, FRADU, 1975
Light Aircraft Grey overall with areas of Fluorescent Orange-Red ('DayGlo'). Note Harley light installation at tip of nose

Hunter T.8M XL580, No 899 Naval Air Squadron, 1985
Extra Dark Sea Grey over White. Note the 899 Squadron 'winged fist' emblem on fin.
This aircraft was a Sea Harrier radar trainer
Inset: No 899 NAS 'winged fist' emblem

Colour Art © Srecko Bradic

Hunter F.6 N-222, No 325 Squadron Koninklijke Luchtmacht (KLu), mid-60s
Dark Green and Dark Sea Grey over High Speed Silver. Squadron emblem is a black scorpion on a
yellow circle – see scrap view for detail. Serial in white on nose, repeated smaller on fin. Aircraft later
sold to Qatar – see later profile

Hunter FR.71A, J732, Grupo 9, Chilean Air Force, 1970s
Dark Green and Dark Sea Grey over High Speed Silver. Blue rudder with white star. Serial number '732'
in black on rear fuselage. Note small Grupo 9 badge on nose

Hunter F.56, BA341, No 14 Squadron, Indian Air Force 1970
Camouflage is a faded Dark Green and Dark Sea Grey over High Speed Silver scheme. Rudder possibly
Indian roundel green. Arrowhead on rear fuselage was possibly saffron edged with white. Squadron
emblem of red bull on white disc seen on nose

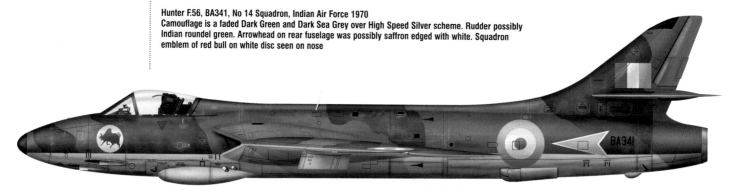

Hunter T.66 S573, 'Indian Banners' Squadron, 1995
Camouflage scheme appears to be faded Light Aircraft Grey with Dark Green disruptive pattern over
Aluminium under surfaces. 'Banners Squadron' emblem on nose in light red and mid green with Hunter
silhouette

Colour Art © Srecko Bradic

Colour Side-views • 9

Hunter FGA.9 810/L, No 2 Squadron, Royal Jordanian Air Force, 1967
Dark Green and Dark Sea Grey over High Speed Silver. No 2 Sqn used black and white checks on nose,
wingtips and rudder. The squadron emblem is a black falcon on white disc. White code letter 'L' on fin

Hunter F.78 QA-12, Qatar Emiri Air Force, circa 1970s
Export desert camouflage is Brown ICI F407-1815, Sand ICI F407-1814 and Deep Sky Blue ICI F407-
1813.
See notes on export camouflage elsewhere in this book

Hunter F.74 515, No 140 Squadron, Republic of Singapore Air Force
Dark Green BS 641, Dark Earth BS 450 and Middle Bronze Green BS 223 over pale grey, (possibly FS
36622). Contrast between the greens is low and does not show up well in b/w photos. Red/black checks
on rudder and nose.
Scrap view: No 140 Sqn emblem of an osprey's legs over a map of Singapore Island – legs red and
yellow, island in green

Hunter FGA.70 L-284, Lebanese Air Force, 2008
Dark Green and Dark Sea Grey over High Speed Silver. No individual markings have been seen on these
reactivated aircraft to date

Colour Art © Srecko Bradic

Hunter F.58 ZZ191, Hawker Hunter Aviation under contract to Royal Air Force, 2008
Dark Green and Dark Sea Grey over Light Aircraft Grey. Company logo carried behind canopy reads
'Hawker Hunter Aviation' and features six white stars on blue background. Slogan on spine reads
'www.hunterteam.com'

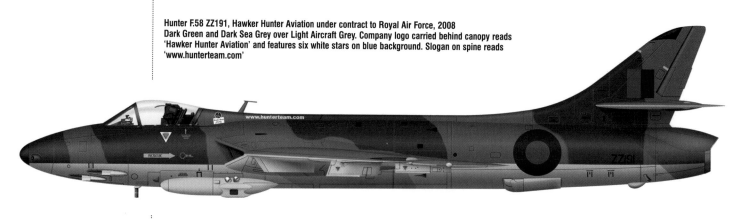

Hunter F.50 34083/33, F9, Swedish Air Force, Sweden, 1961
NATO Dark Green over light blue-grey. Note nose band in Swedish roundel blue, tail code '33' in white,
squadron identity code '9' in yellow on rear fuselage

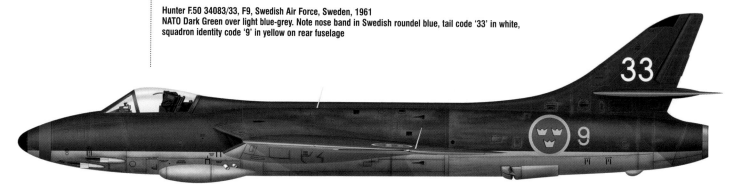

Hunter FGA.9 R286, No 1 Squadron, Rhodesian Air Force, 1974
Overall Dark Earth BS650 with disruptive upper surface pattern of Dark Green BS641

Hunter F.51 E-401, Esk 724, Royal Danish Air Force, 1973
Overall matt NATO Dark Green which faded to an uneven olive drab finish. Serial number E-401 in black
on nose

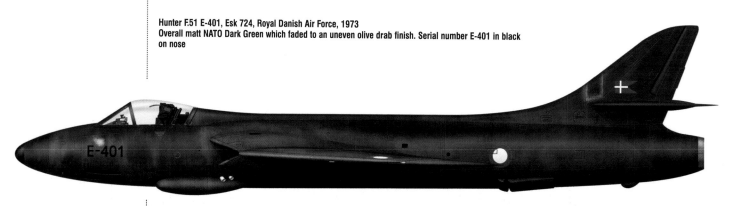

Colour Art © Srecko Bradic

Colour Side-views • 11

Hunter FGA.80 803, Kenyan Air Force, 1978
Dark Green and Dark Sea Grey over High Speed Silver. Serial number in black on rear fuselage

Hunter FGA.59 575, Iraqi Air Force, 1964
Dark Green and Dark Sea Grey over High Speed Silver. Serial in white Arabic numerals on rear fuselage

Hunter F.60 60-603, No 6 Squadron, Royal Saudi AF, 1966
Brown ICI F407-1815 and Sand ICI F407-1814 over Deep Sky Blue ICI F407-1813. Serials, on nose and on the fin above tailplanes, titles, fin flash and roundels all in bright green

Hunter FGA.76 702, Abu Dhabi Army Air Wing, 1970
Brown ICI F407-1815 and Sand ICI F407-1814 over Deep Sky Blue ICI F407-1813. Note the red cheat line along the fuselage demarcation

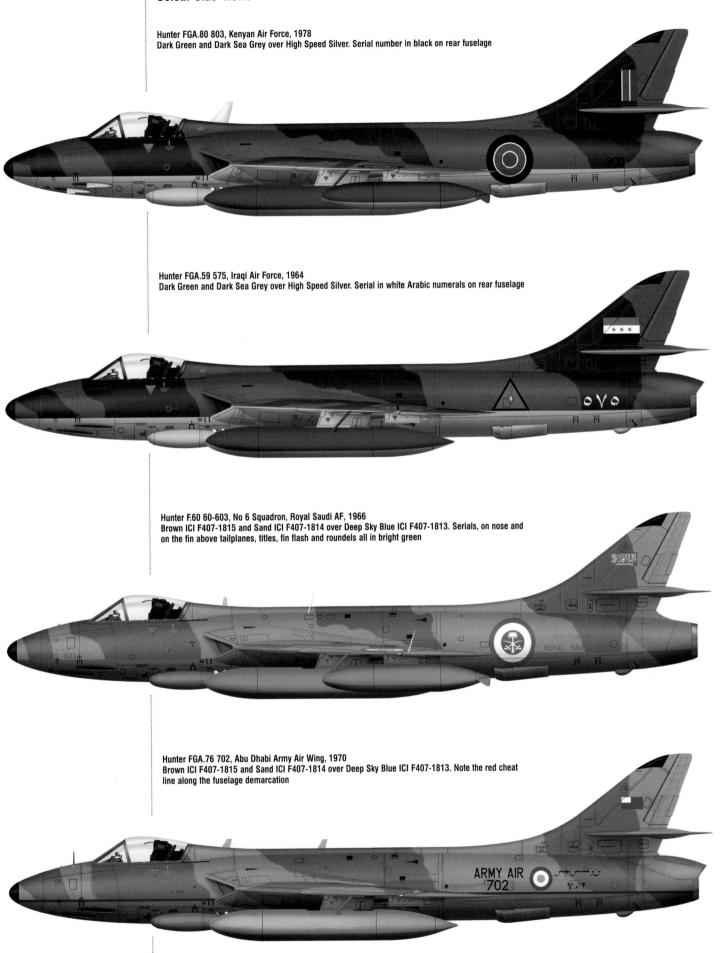

Colour Art © Srecko Bradic

Hunter FGA.57 212, Kuwaiti Air Force, 1965
Brown ICI F407-1815, Sand ICI F407-1814 and Deep Sky Blue ICI F407-1813

Hunter FGA.76 CC705, Somali Democratic Republican Air Force, 1992
A very weathered Brown ICI F407-1815 and Sand ICI F407-1814 over Deep Sky Blue ICI F407-1813.
Note the red cheat line on fuselage. A former-Abu Dhabi Air Force machine, CC705 was derelict at the
time it was recorded for illustration here, but Hunter camouflage was the same throughout its career in
Somalia

Hunter F.58 J-4015, Swiss Air Force, 1970s
Standard Dark Green and Dark Sea Grey over High Speed Silver camouflage modified with the Dark Sea
Grey areas overpainted in a temporary white finish for winter camouflage trials

Hunter F.73 847 of the Sultan of Oman Air Force, 1980s
Camouflage scheme is light blue-grey overall with dark blue-grey disruptive pattern – the exact shades
of which are unknown, which in any case were very badly faded and weathered. Note the small Omani
shield insignia on the fin was only national markingcarried

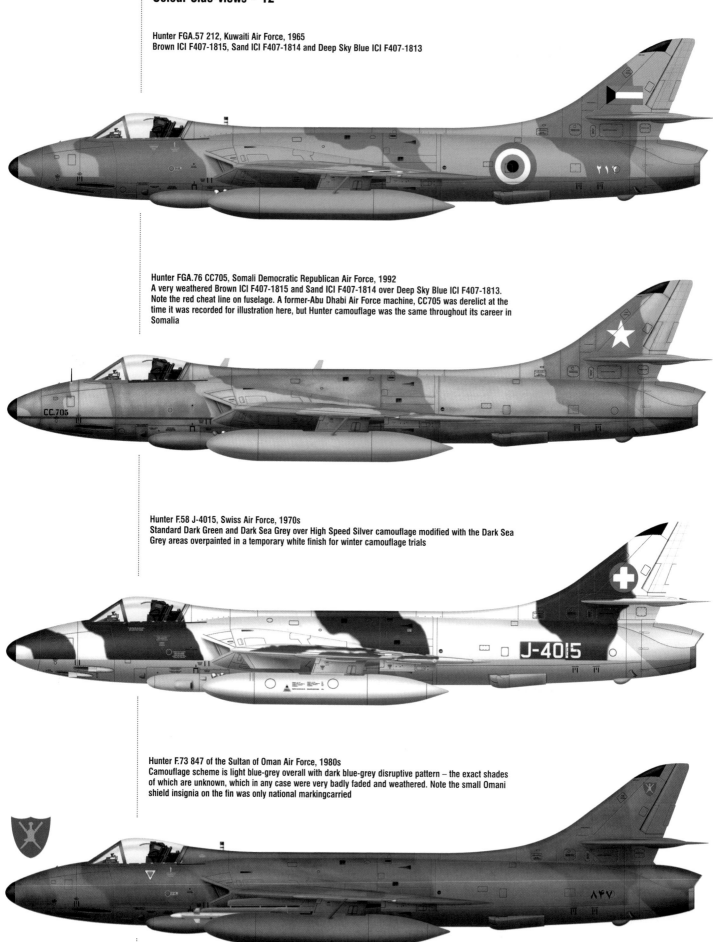

Colour Art © Srecko Bradic

Colour Side-views • 13

Hunter F.6 XG159/N, No 92 Squadron 'Blue Diamonds' aerobatic team, 1961
Overall gloss Aircraft Blue BS 108 with white trim and wingtips. Red/yelloe squadron bars on nose
flanking squadron emblem of pale green/yellow snake and red leaf on a white disk. Note roundels and
fin flash outlined in white. Serial and code letter 'N' above fin flash in black

Hunter F.6 XF506/X, No 111 Squadron 'Black Arrows', 1958
Overall gloss black. All roundels outlined in white, as well as leading/trailing edges only of fin flash. Serial and
code letter 'X' above fin flash in red. Legend on nose reads 'SQN LDR P A LATHAM AFC' in yellow, over
squadron bars and badge in standard frame, with Squadron Leader's pennant underneath

Hunter F.6 IF-80, 'Diables Rouge', Belgian Air Force, 1960
Overall gloss bright red with white fuselage trim line. Squadron emblem is a yellow lion rampant on
black shield, outlined in yellow. Roundels have thin dark blue outline. Note serial number in white
immediately under the tailplane

Hunter F.56 A463/3, No 20 Squadron 'Thunderbolts', Indian Air Force, 1990
Overall dark blue with white lightning flashes along the fuselage, wings and tail. Aircraft code numeral
'3' in saffron on top of fin. Serial in black on rear fuselage. Squadron number in black on white disc on
the nose

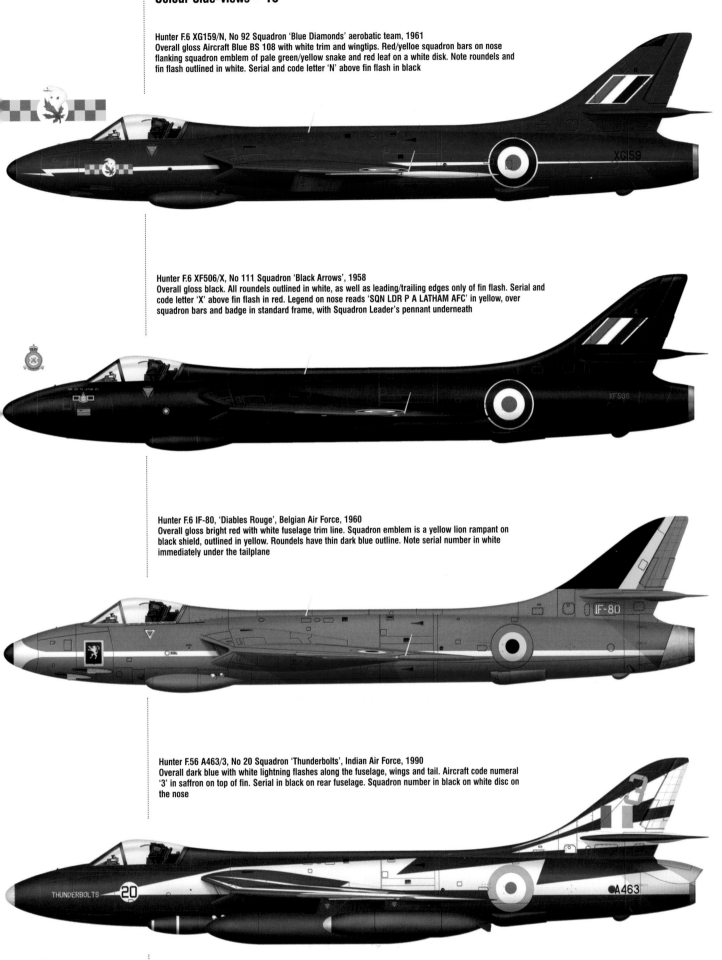

Colour Art © Srecko Bradic

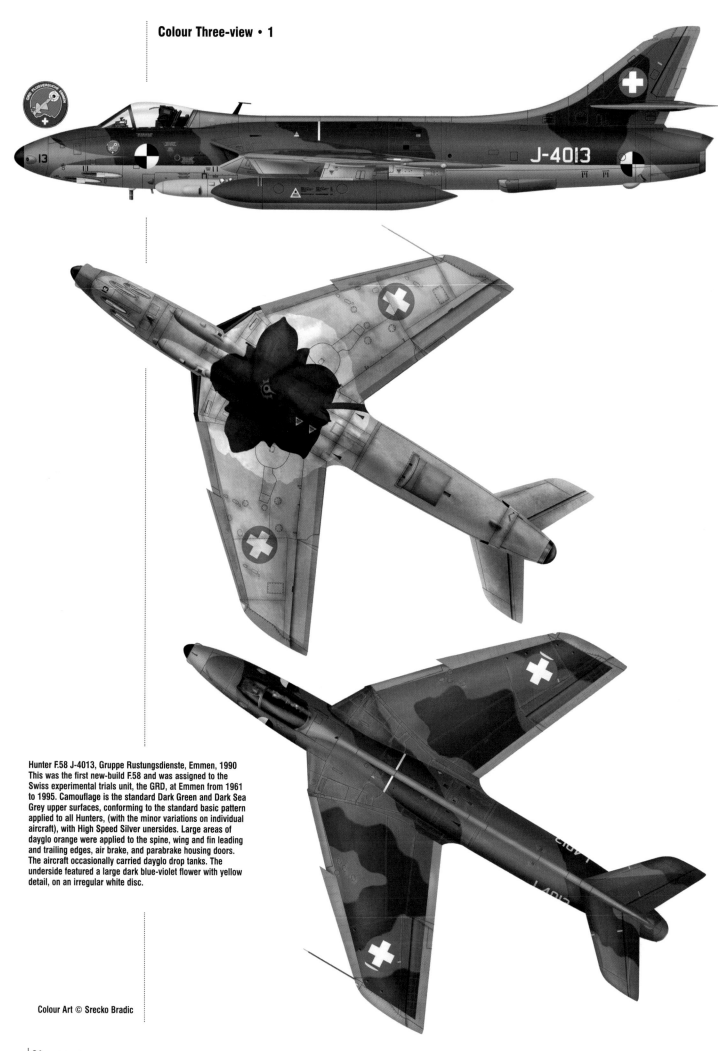

Hunter F.58 J-4013, Gruppe Rustungsdienste, Emmen, 1990
This was the first new-build F.58 and was assigned to the
Swiss experimental trials unit, the GRD, at Emmen from 1961
to 1995. Camouflage is the standard Dark Green and Dark Sea
Grey upper surfaces, conforming to the standard basic pattern
applied to all Hunters, (with the minor variations on individual
aircraft), with High Speed Silver unersides. Large areas of
dayglo orange were applied to the spine, wing and fin leading
and trailing edges, air brake, and parabrake housing doors.
The aircraft occasionally carried dayglo drop tanks. The
underside featured a large dark blue-violet flower with yellow
detail, on an irregular white disc.

Colour Art © Srecko Bradic

Hunter
Walkaround

Presented here is a selection of detail photos of various Hunters – as most Hunter airframes were the same, many of these details are applicable for most marks. All photos by author unless noted.

Cockpit

F.4 cockpit forward view
(© Mark Gauntlett with thanks to Mark Templeman)

F.4 cockpit overview
(© Mark Gauntlett with thanks to Mark Templeman)

F.4 port side
(© Mark Gauntlett with thanks to Mark Templeman)

F.4 starboard side
(© Mark Gauntlett with thanks to Mark Templeman)

FGA.9 cockpit overview. XE601
(© Mark Gauntlett with thanks to SkyBlue Aviation & Hunter Flying)

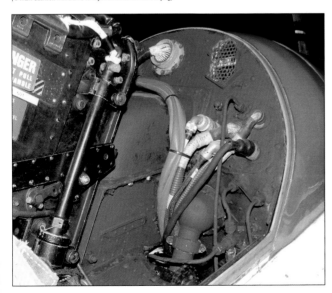

Behind the seat, port side of XE601
(© Mark Gauntlett with thanks to SkyBlue Aviation & Hunter Flying)

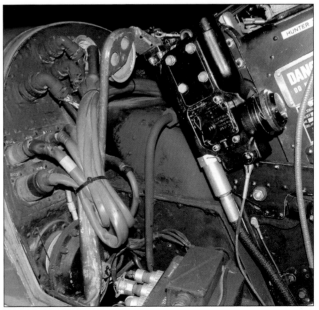

The area behind the seat, starboard side of XE601
(© Mark Gauntlett with thanks to SkyBlue Aviation & Hunter Flying)

T.7 XL569 overview *(© John Davidson)*

T.7 pilot's main panel *(© John Davidson)*

T.7 pilot's port panel *(© John Davidson)*

T.7 pilot's side panel *(© John Davidson)*

T.7 co-pilot's main panel *(© John Davidson)*

T.7 co-pilot's side panel *(© John Davidson)*

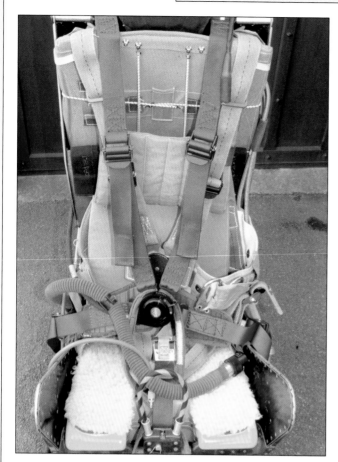

MB Mk.2H head box port side *(© Mark Gauntlett)*

MB Mk.2H harnesses *(© Mark Gauntlett)*

MB Mk.2H head box starboard side *(© Mark Gauntlett)*

F.6 port canopy view *(© Greg Wilson)*

F.4 looking down on seat and starboard panels *(© Mark Gauntlett)*

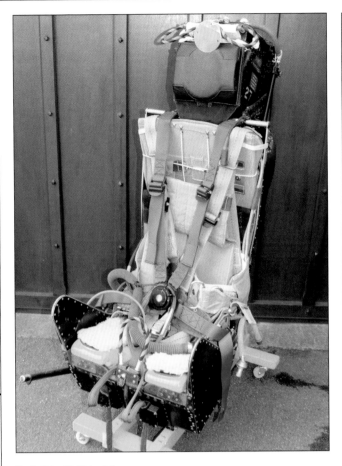

Martin-Baker Mk.2H front view *(© Mark Gauntlett)*

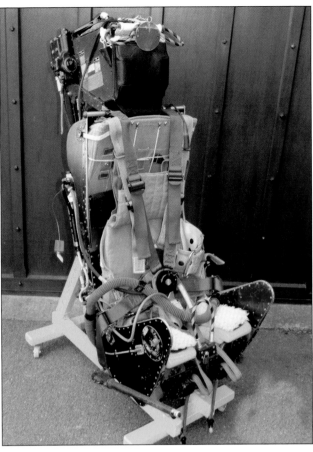

MB Mk.2H front view *(© Mark Gauntlett)*

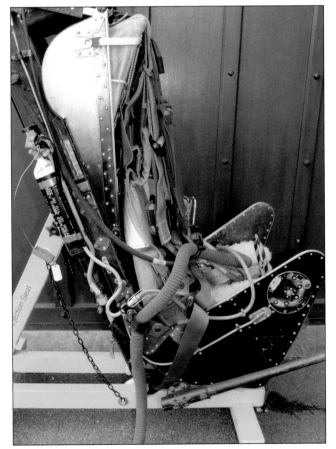

MB Mk.2H starboard side view *(© Mark Gauntlett)*

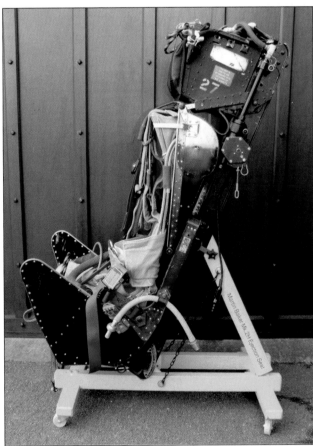

MB Mk.2H port side view *(© Mark Gauntlett)*

Cutaway of an Avon 200. While this is from a Lightning, the basic core of the engine is very similar to that used by the Hunter (© John Davidson)

Close-up of the splitter

Overall view of intake area. This was usually a dirty grey in colour

Side view of the splitter plate with stencilling info (© Greg Wilson)

Same Avon 200 from another angle *(© John Davidson)*

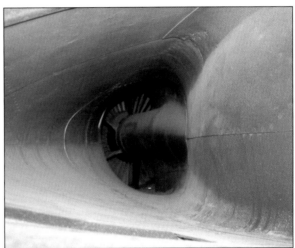

View deeper inside the intake of the compressor fan

Intake duct

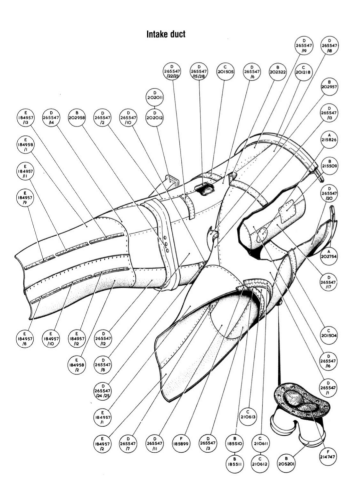

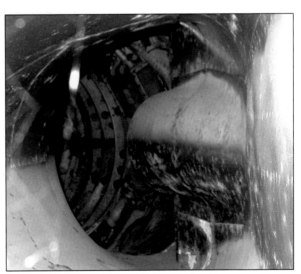

This airframe – F.1 WT619 – was sectioned by the IWM and was until recently on display in Manchester. It has now moved to IWM Cosford *(© John Davidson)*

Forward fuselage and cockpit area *(© John Davidson)*

Centre fuselage and inner wing *(© John Davidson)*

Wing and centre fuselage from overhead *(© Greg Wilson)*

Tail section and rear fuselage *(© John Davidson)*

Overview of wing *(© John Davidson)*

Well dressed Hunter pilot, 1950s-60s *(© Mark Gauntlett)*
This is the 1950s-1960s style kit and consists of:

- Blue cloth Type G flying helmet – contains earphones, socket for connection to microphone and down lead to connect to mic-tel connector on ejection seat.
- Mark 1A 'bone-dome'. Basically a 'shell' with webbing lining to fit over the Type G helmet. This allowed the Type G to be worn alone if required by crew of certain aircraft e.g. V-bomber 'back seaters'. Initially supplied in silver (later in olive green or grey) but often repainted (e.g. in white) by individual squadrons. If repainted then squadron badges were often applied as well. The single visor, which could be positioned at a number of points along the central track, was supplied in a number of different tints.
- Type A-13 oxygen mask which contains a rigid metal exoskeleton and tensioning frame. In an emergency the frame could be instantly tightened (by means of a toggle lever on the front) against the face to enhance the seal. The WWII-vintage Type H oxygen mask was also used during this time period in the Hunter.
- Mk.2 flying suit. This is the later type of blue suit (earlier versions being a darker grey-blue colour) and has provision for ejection seat leg garters to be stitched inside the legs. In reality external garters, as pictured, were more often worn. The anti-g suit was worn under the flying suit with only the air supply tube protruding near the left hip.

- Orange cotton life preserver made by the Frankenstein Company of Manchester. The garment contained a rubber bladder inflated by pulling down on a release knob mounted, along with the CO_2 bottle, under the left side of the stole. Pockets contained the SARBE search and rescue beacon (more commonly referred to as a PLB - Personal Locator Beacon - nowadays), whistle, light, heliograph, survival kit etc.
- 1953 pattern flying boots. Similar to the wartime 'escape' pattern boots in appearance with loose calf section and distinct 'shoe' lower section.
- Light grey kid leather flying gloves.

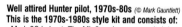

Well attired Hunter pilot, 1970s-80s *(© Mark Gauntlett)*
This is the 1970s-1980s style kit and consists of:

- Mark 3C helmet. The Mk.3 series superseded the Mk.2 (also worn by Hunter pilots) and was the first RAF flying helmet with dual visors. The inner, clear, visor was fitted with a catch to lock the visor in the down position. The outer, dark, visor could be positioned in any position. Usually seen in gloss white or matt green.
- Type Q oxygen mask. This, along with the identical but larger size Type P, became the standard mask of the RAF and is still in use today. It too is fitted with an external rigid exoskeleton and tensioning frame, is attached to hooks on the helmet by means of chains and adjusted for fit using the knurled, gold coloured, nuts on each side.
- Mk.7A lightweight flying suit. The suit illustrated here is the lightweight version of one of the many designs used by the RAF during this period. Although it appears externally similar to the standard suit, it is made from a very lightweight cotton material and was worn by aircrew in hotter climates. It contains sleeve pockets for pencils as well as large knee pockets for note boards, maps etc.
- Anti-g suit. The air supply pipe protruding from the left side of the waist band connected to the anti-g air pipe on the side of the ejection seat pan. In the Hunter air for the anti-g system is contained in two spherical bottles mounted in the cockpit behind the seat.
- Green nylon Mk.17 life preserver. This version contained an orange bladder completely contained within the green nylon stole. The stole was closed around its edge by means of a frangible plastic rod which shattered when the jacket inflated to release the expanding bladder. Inflation was initiated by pulling the black beaded handle on the front left side of the stole. Pockets contained Personal Locator Beacon, emergency flying rations, survival equipment etc. The connector hanging from the front of the life preserver connects to the lowering line on the PSP (Personal Survival Pack) in the seat pan.
- 1969 pattern flying boots. This design dispensed with the loose calf section of the 1953 pattern, in favour of a more familiar boot design, and is laced right to the top. The same basic design is still in use today.
- Blue ejection seat leg garters.
- Light grey kid leather flying gloves. Also available in green and black.

General overview of ex-Swiss F.58, J-4035

Port nose view

Starboard nose view

The small hole over the nose is for the gun camera

The radome for the gun laying radar is held in place with screws. The lump is associated with the Swiss RWR system

With the nose cone removed, the front bulkhead can be seen, although most of the fittings are **missing** (© John Adams)

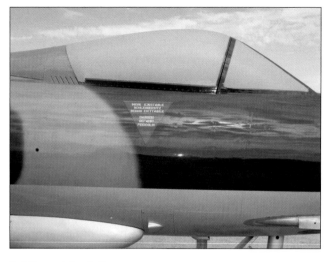

Cockpit area, starboard side

Port view of F.1 nose *(© James Perrin)*

General view of port forward fuselage - this is an F.1 *(© James Perrin)*

Close-up of the rear of the canopy *(© Greg Wilson)*

Access panels top

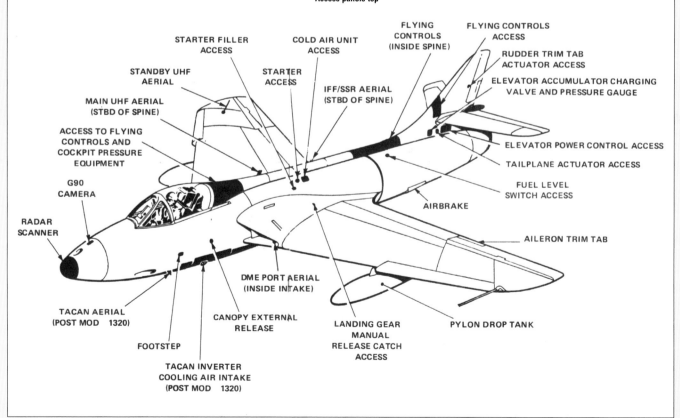

STARTER FILLER
ACCESS

COLD AIR UNIT
ACCESS

FLYING
CONTROLS
(INSIDE SPINE)

FLYING CONTROLS
ACCESS

STANDBY UHF
AERIAL

STARTER
ACCESS

RUDDER TRIM TAB
ACTUATOR ACCESS

MAIN UHF AERIAL
(STBD OF SPINE)

IFF/SSR AERIAL
(STBD OF SPINE)

ELEVATOR ACCUMULATOR CHARGING
VALVE AND PRESSURE GAUGE

ACCESS TO FLYING
CONTROLS AND
COCKPIT PRESSURE
EQUIPMENT

ELEVATOR POWER CONTROL ACCESS

TAILPLANE ACTUATOR ACCESS

G90
CAMERA

FUEL LEVEL
SWITCH ACCESS

RADAR
SCANNER

AIRBRAKE

AILERON TRIM TAB

DME PORT AERIAL
(INSIDE INTAKE)

TACAN AERIAL
(POST MOD 1320)

CANOPY EXTERNAL
RELEASE

LANDING GEAR
MANUAL
RELEASE CATCH
ACCESS

PYLON DROP TANK

FOOTSTEP

TACAN INVERTER
COOLING AIR INTAKE
(POST MOD 1320)

This view better shows the canopy rail *(© Greg Wilson)*

Plain gun troughs as often seen on earlier marks *(© Greg Wilson)*

Detail of gun troughs with gun blast deflectors detail – note the deflectors are welded to the skin

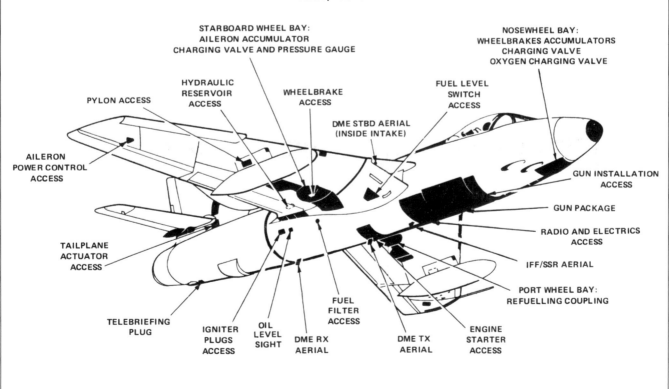

Note the slots on the undersides of the deflectors *(© Greg Wilson)*

Access panels under

STARBOARD WHEEL BAY:
AILERON ACCUMULATOR
CHARGING VALVE AND PRESSURE GAUGE

NOSEWHEEL BAY:
WHEELBRAKES ACCUMULATORS
CHARGING VALVE
OXYGEN CHARGING VALVE

HYDRAULIC
RESERVOIR
ACCESS

WHEELBRAKE
ACCESS

FUEL LEVEL
SWITCH
ACCESS

PYLON ACCESS

DME STBD AERIAL
(INSIDE INTAKE)

AILERON
POWER CONTROL
ACCESS

GUN INSTALLATION
ACCESS

GUN PACKAGE

RADIO AND ELECTRICS
ACCESS

TAILPLANE
ACTUATOR
ACCESS

IFF/SSR AERIAL

PORT WHEEL BAY:
REFUELLING COUPLING

TELEBRIEFING
PLUG

IGNITER
PLUGS
ACCESS

OIL
LEVEL
SIGHT

FUEL
FILTER
ACCESS

DME RX
AERIAL

DME TX
AERIAL

ENGINE
STARTER
ACCESS

Centre fuselage

Front fuselage

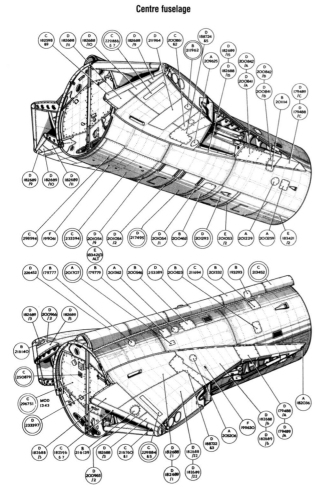

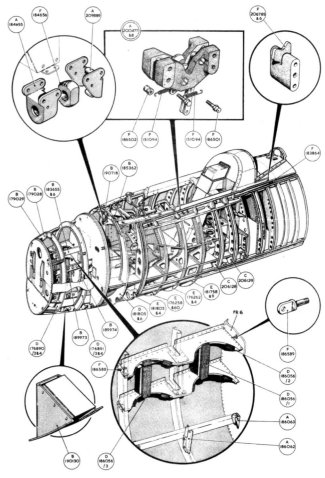

General intake view. The trough on the upper wing surface is a boundary layer air outlet. The small rectangular panel behind the upper lip is an automatic bleed air door

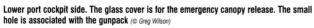

Lower port cockpit side. The glass cover is for the emergency canopy release. The small hole is associated with the gunpack (© Greg Wilson)

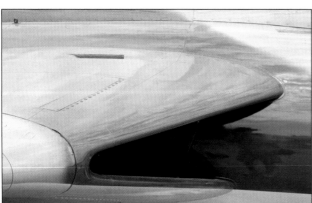

Note the lack of rear canopy frame on the Hunter (© Greg Wilson)

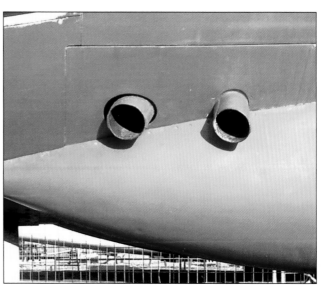

Rear end of the link collector tank, colloquially known as 'Sabrinas'. Note the tubular cartridge case ejector chutes (© Greg Wilson)

Underside of the front end of the Sabrina; note the cooling air intake *(© Greg Wilson)*

Access hatches for the front of the gun bay *(© Greg Wilson)*

General Arrangement

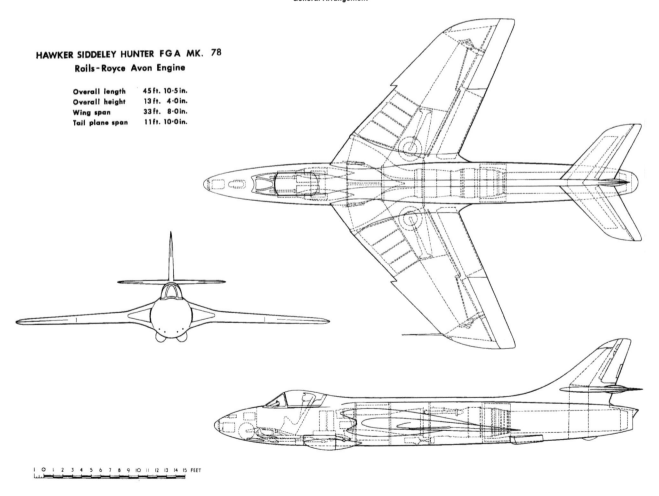

HAWKER SIDDELEY HUNTER FGA MK. 78
Rolls-Royce Avon Engine

Overall length	45 ft. 10·5 in.
Overall height	13 ft. 4·0 in.
Wing span	33 ft. 8·0 in.
Tail plane span	11 ft. 10·0 in.

1 0 1 2 3 4 5 6 7 8 9 10 11 12 13 14 15 FEET

Hood and windscreen

Anti-icer system

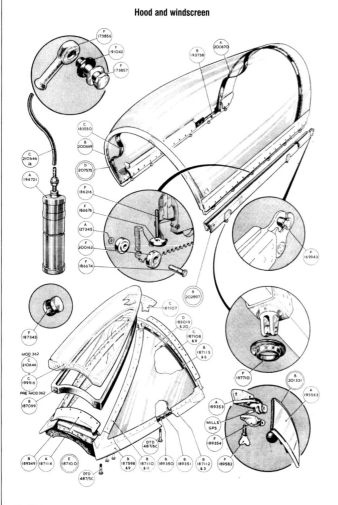

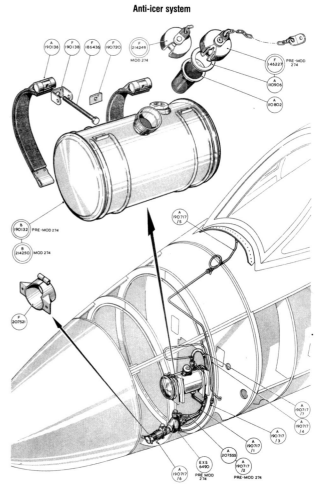

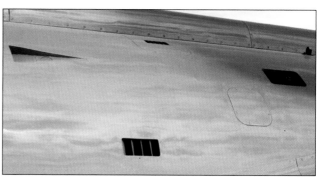

General upper fuselage view. Note how smoothly the inner wing contours blend into the fuselage

Close-up of the various intakes and exhausts on the centre fuselage - this arrangement is applicable for the Avon 200-series

The circular vent aft of the wing trailing edge is an engine cool air outlet

Same view shows typical arrangement of an Avon 100-series airframe, in this case an F.51 *(© Greg Wilson)*

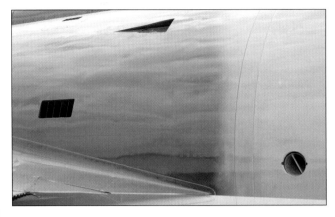

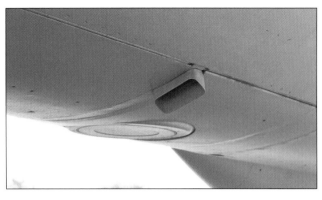

Port fuselage view – note the various vents and intakes are the same on both sides of the engine compartment

Underside, just aft of the Sabrinas. The circular panel on the engine starter access door is a landing light on the F.58 only. The vent is the engine starter exhaust

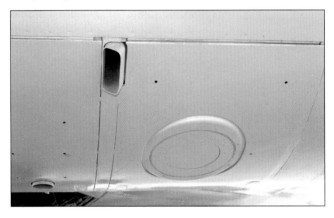

Underside, just aft of the Sabrinas. The circular panel on the engine starter access door is a landing light on the F.58 only. The vent is the engine starter exhaust

Underside. Note NACA intakes

Blanks and picketing

Ground locks

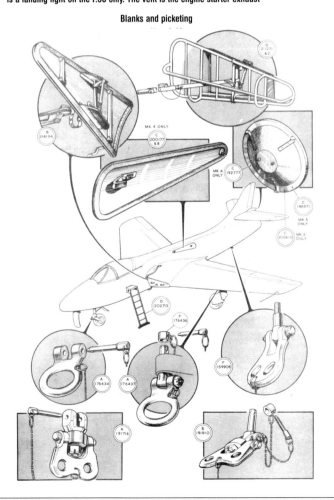

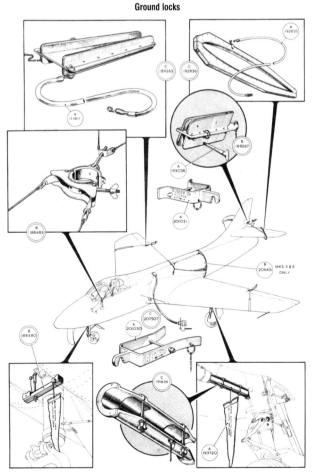

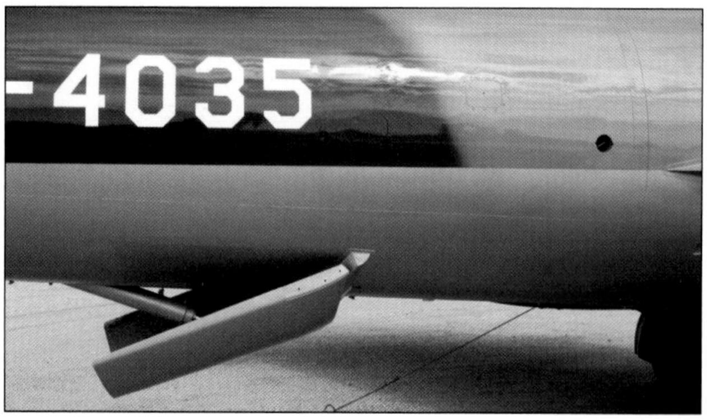

Rear fuselage aspect. The twin panel lines just aft of the trailing edge are the rear transport joint – the fuselage is detachable at the point to aid in engine change/service. Note the position of the air brake fairing

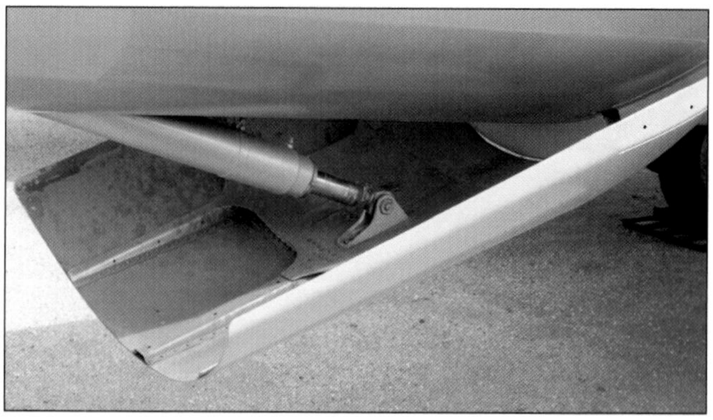

Air brake. This would normally be closed when the aircraft is on the ground, but will droop with a loss of hydraulic system pressure over time

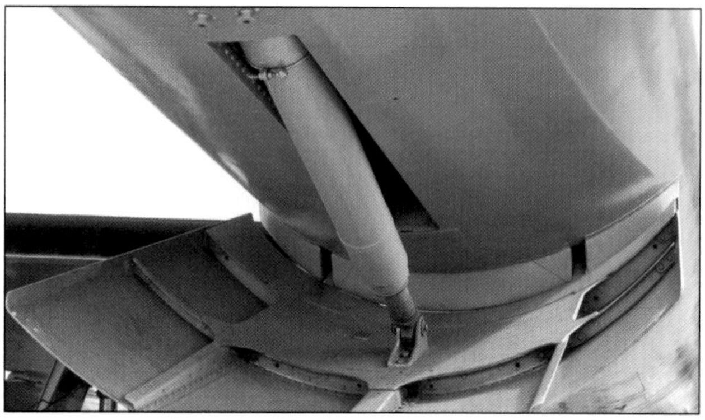

Air brake interior. Note the internal strengthening plate

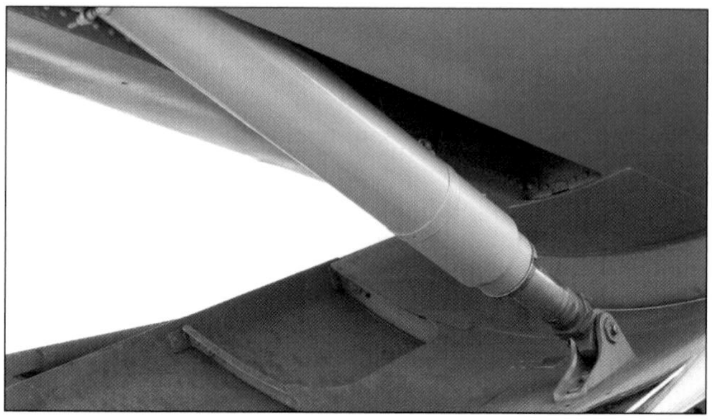

Close-up of the retraction strut and mount

Packing Dims (FGA)

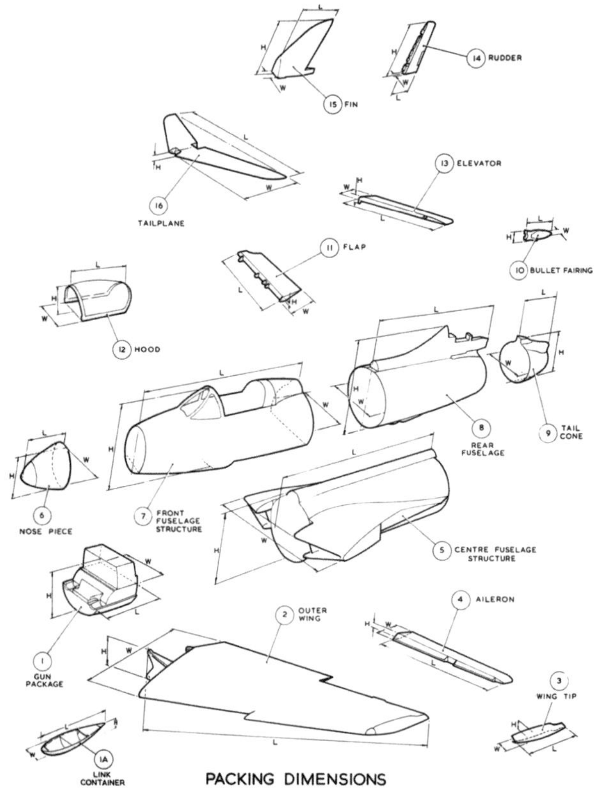

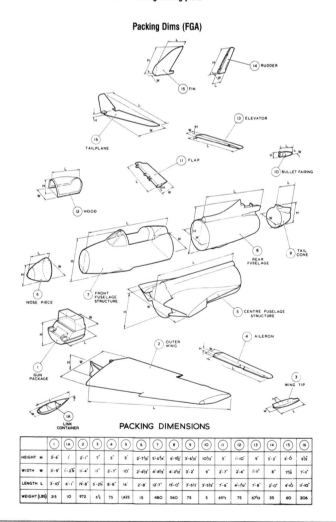

PACKING DIMENSIONS

	1	1A	2	3	4	5	6	7	8	9	10	11	12	13	14	15	16
HEIGHT H	3'-6"	1'	2'-1"	7"	5"	5"	2'-7½"	5'-6¾"	6'-9½"	3'-6½"	10½"	5"	1'-10"	9"	5'-2"	6'-0"	6½"
WIDTH W	3'-9"	1'-2¾"	11'-4"	11"	2'-7"	10'	2'-4½"	4'-8½"	4'-2½"	3'-2"	9"	2'-7"	2'-4"	1'-11"	8"	7½"	7'-11"
LENGTH L	3'-10"	6'-1"	19'-8"	5'-2¼"	8'-8"	16'	2'-8"	12'-7"	15'-0"	3'-6½"	3'-5½"	7'-6"	4'-1½"	7'-8"	2'-0"	4'-10"	11'-10"
WEIGHT (LBS)	315	10	972	6½	75	1,425	15	480	560	75	5	69½	75	67½	35	60	206

Packing Dims (FR)

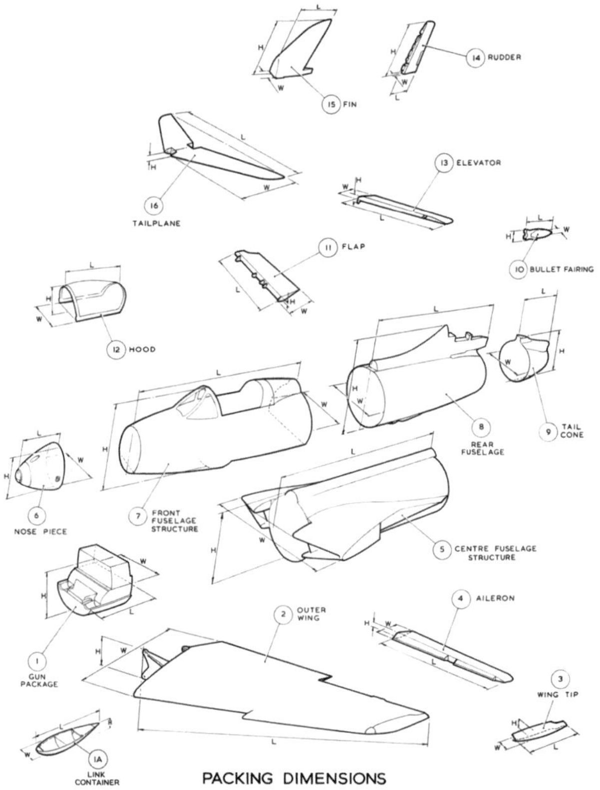

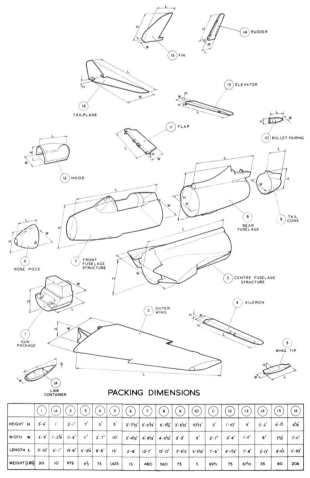

PACKING DIMENSIONS

	1	1A	2	3	4	5	6	7	8	9	10	11	12	13	14	15	16
HEIGHT H	3'-6"	1'	2'-1"	7"	5"	5"	2'-7½"	5'-6¾"	6'-9½"	3'-6½"	10½"	5"	1'-10"	9"	5'-2"	6'-0"	6½"
WIDTH W	3'-9"	1'-2¾"	11'-4"	11"	2'-7"	10'	2'-4½"	4'-8½"	4'-2½"	3'-2"	9"	2'-7"	2'-4"	1'-11"	8"	7½"	7'-11"
LENGTH L	3'-10"	6'-1"	19'-8"	5'-2¼"	8'-8"	16'	2'-8"	12'-7"	15'-0"	3'-6½"	3'-5½"	7'-6"	4'-1½"	7'-8"	2'-0"	4'-10"	11'-10"
WEIGHT (LBS)	315	10	972	6½	75	1,425	15	480	560	75	5	69½	75	67½	35	60	206

Tail cone (FGA)

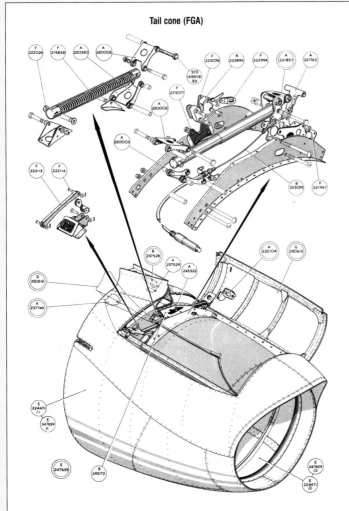

Rear fuselage (FGA)

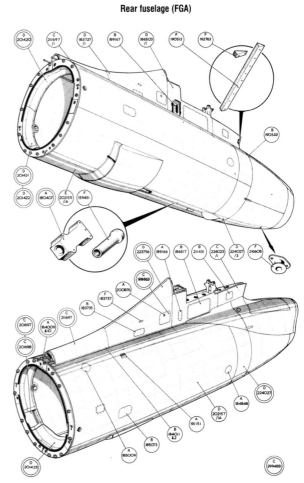

Airbrake in closed position *(© Greg Wilson)*

Close-up of the tail cone and above that the brake parachute housing. You can just make out the outline of the starboard door for this

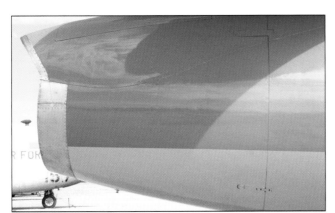

Side view of the tail cone. Note the tabs for the latches, used when the tail cone is removed

Side view of F.51 tail area *(© Greg Wilson)*

Rear view of F.1 tailcone – note the sharp upsweep of the ventral lines close to the orifice of this Avon 100-series *(© John Adams)*

Port view of F.1 tailcone *(© John Adams)*

Port view of FGA.9 tailcone. Note missing elevator booster access panel *(© Greg Wilson)*

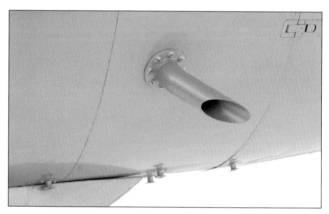

Fuel vent, on the port lower fuselage, just ahead of the tailcone joint

Tail bumper – note the roller

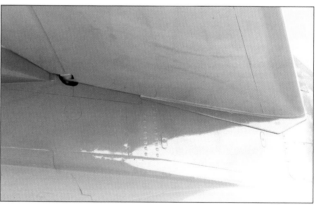

Underside of variable incidence tailplane. Note the hole for the hinge, and the swivel plate

Forward fin, F.51. Small square panel in centre is the hydraulic accumulator access
(© Greg Wilson)

Underside of starboard tailplane

The anti-buffet bullet behind the tailplane. Note the streamlined navigation light cover at the tip. The lumps are associated with the Swiss RWR system

Overall view of the fin and tailplanes

View of the underside of the parabrake fairing, with its smooth surface. Tailcone diameter of this Avon 200-series airframe is 62cm/25ins

Close-up of top of fin and rudder *(© Mark Gauntlett)*

Stencilling guide

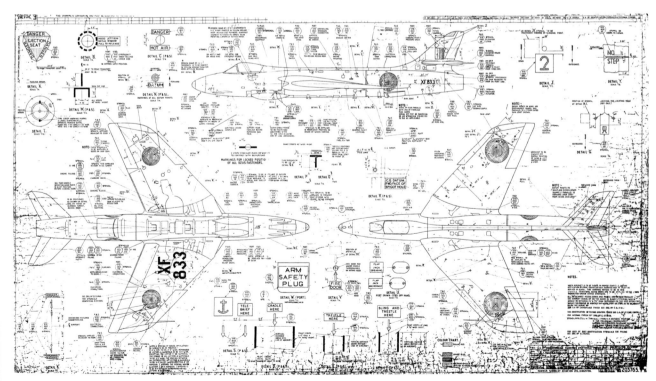

Starboard dog-tooth extension

Port flap

Close up of outboard section

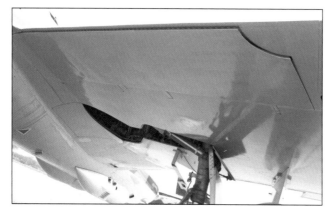

Starboard flap. Note the outboard cut-out for inner pylon drop tank clearance

Starboard wingtip, including light cover, here covered by a non-service protective coating

Original flap

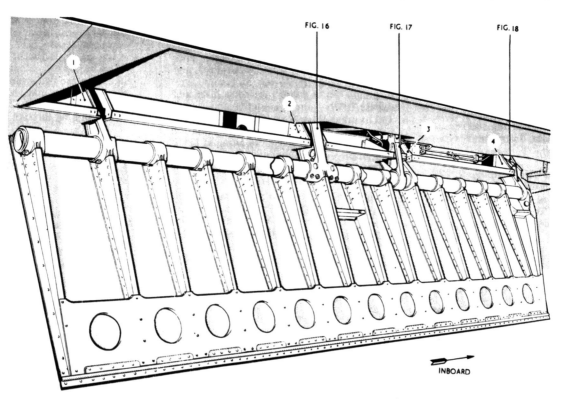

Close-up of the upper surface of port flap

Starboard outer wing undersides – note the rocket hardpoint mounts and outer pylon

T.7 wing leading edge *(© John Adams)*

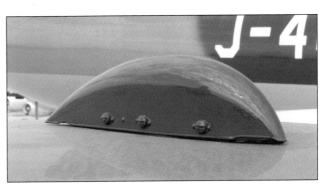

Starboard outer pylon ejector housing

Complete port flap in full down position *(© Greg Wilson)*

Wings

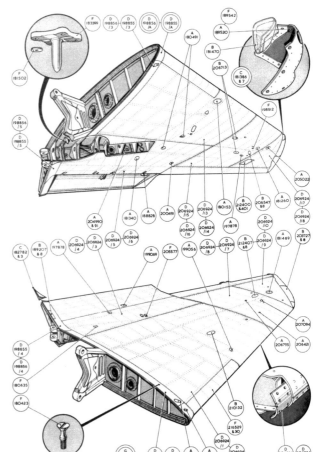

F.1 wing leading edge *(© John Adams)*

View of the nose leg from the rear. Note the link rods attached to leg and door *(© Greg Wilson)*

View of nose leg. Note the scalloped area at the top of the door. The piece of pipe wedged in the fork is not standard! *(© Greg Wilson)*

View of nose leg. Leg is very uncomplicated *(© Greg Wilson)*

The back of the forward u/c door *(© Greg Wilson)*

The rear portion of the nosewheel bay *(© Greg Wilson)*

Looking up at the roof of the nosewheel bay, this is the battery housing *(© Greg Wilson)*

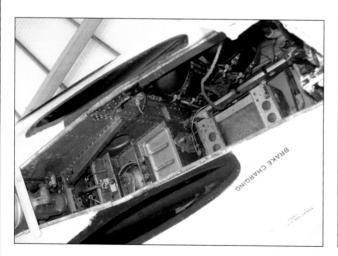

Another view of the nosewheel bay roof. The rear is at the bottom *(© James Perrin)*

Overall view of nose undercarriage *(© John Davidson)*

Maingear doors

Maingear doors

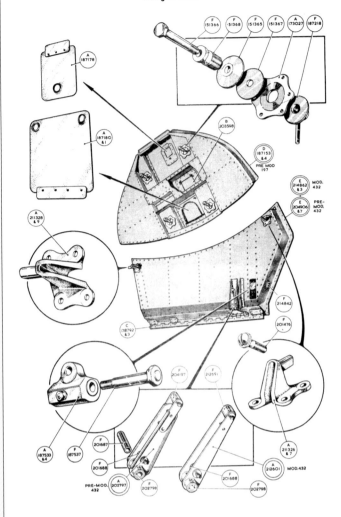

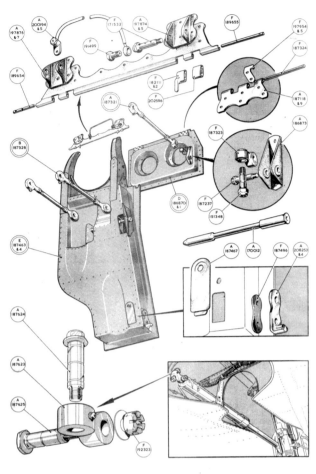

Overall view of main undercarriage, port (© James Perrin)

Port main u/c leg without doors, showing some detail of the back of the leg that usually isn't visible (© Greg Wilson)

Starboard leg shown from straight-on, showing the relationship of the leg to the doors *(© Greg Wilson)*

Port leg – the red bar is non-standard

Starboard leg. The oleo is fully extended on this leg

Port main wheel

Starboard main wheel

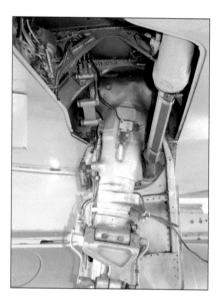

Port leg upper section

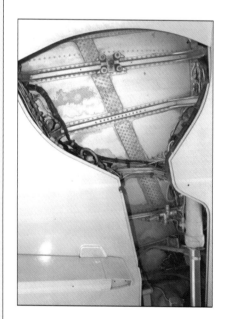

Port main bay roof

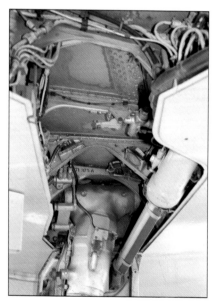

Port main bay and upper leg

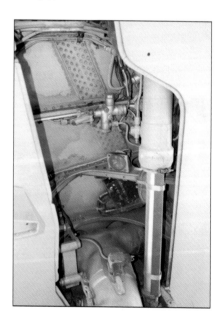

Port main bay and upper leg

Nosegear

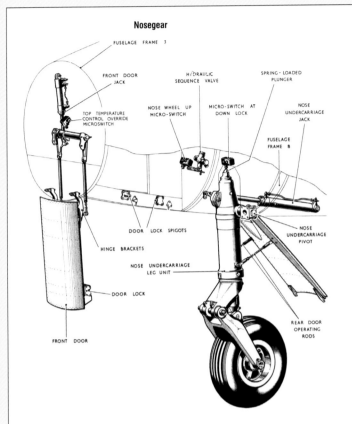

FUSELAGE FRAME 3

FRONT DOOR
JACK

TOP TEMPERATURE
CONTROL OVERRIDE
MICROSWITCH

HYDRAULIC
SEQUENCE VALVE

NOSE WHEEL UP
MICRO-SWITCH

MICRO-SWITCH AT
DOWN LOCK

SPRING - LOADED
PLUNGER

NOSE
UNDERCARRIAGE
JACK

FUSELAGE
FRAME 8

DOOR LOCK SPIGOTS

HINGE BRACKETS

NOSE UNDERCARRIAGE
LEG UNIT

NOSE
UNDERCARRIAGE
PIVOT

DOOR LOCK

REAR DOOR
OPERATING
RODS

FRONT DOOR

Nosegear doors

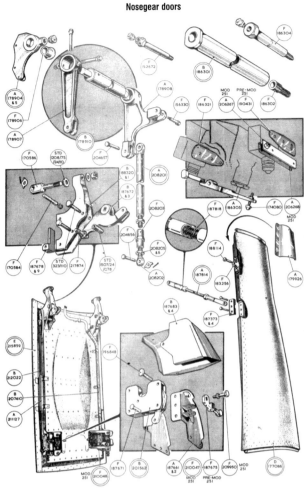

Port main bay, fuselage wall. Note the large single-point refuelling port just ahead of the
door retraction strut *(© Greg Wilson)*

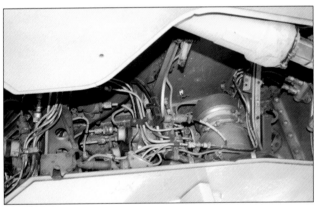

Port main bay

Port main bay. The spike in the top left of the photo engages in the centre of the wheel

Port main bay, looking towards the fuselage area. The inner doors were locked up on
this museum aircraft – not typical of service aircraft

SURA Rockets - pylon-mounted

WING SECTION

SEE ENLARGED VIEW

LAUNCHER RAIL ADAPTER

LAUNCHER RAIL 'B'

Armaments

INBOARD
(*Top to bottom :*)
230 gall. drop tank
100 gall. drop tank
400 kg. bomb
1,000 lb. bomb
200 gall. Napalm bomb
500 lb. bomb
2" Rocket Launcher
6 x 3" R.P.s
2 x 25 lb. Practice bombs

OUTBOARD
(*Top to bottom :*)
100 gall. drop tank
100 gall. Napalm bomb
12 x 3" R.P.s (light heads)
4 x 3" R.P.s (60 lb. heads)
Combinations of
Bofors, T.10,
H.V.A.R., or Oërlikon
Rocket Projectiles

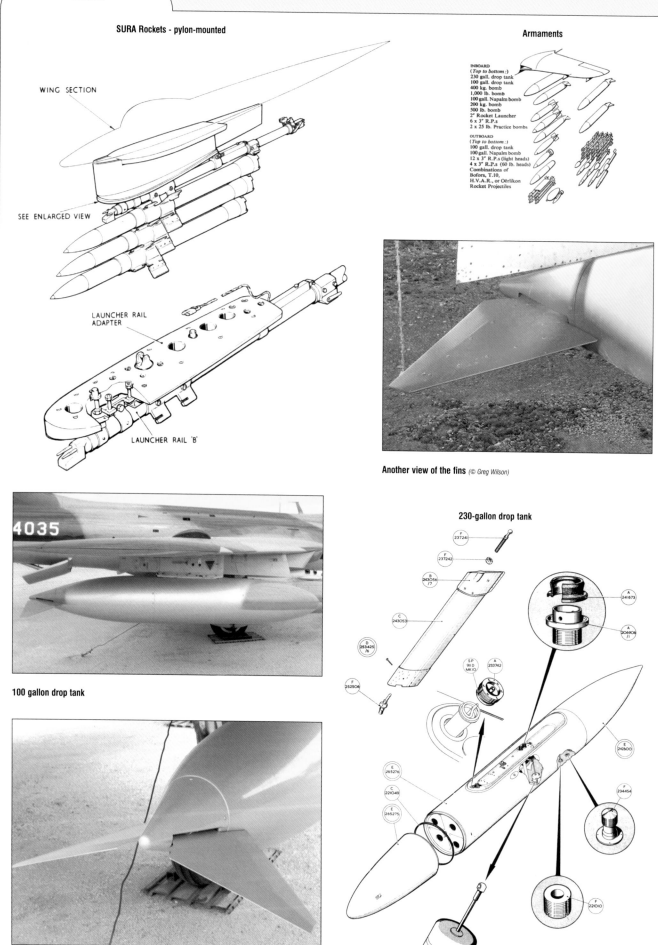

Another view of the fins (© Greg Wilson)

4035

100 gallon drop tank

100 gallon drop tank rear fins

230-gallon drop tank

Gun package

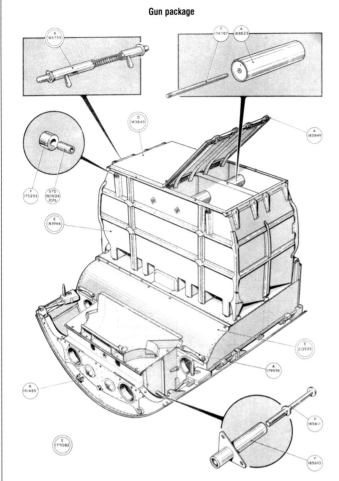

Sabrinas

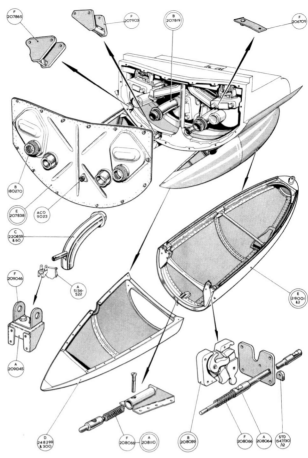

Another view of the outer pylon

Outer pylon

Inner pylon

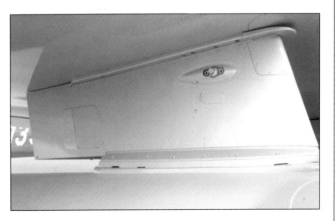

Another view of the inner pylon

Hispano Suiza 'Sura' rockets in a typical Hunter installation *(© courtesy Qatar Emiri Air Force via Mark Gauntlett)*

100 gallon drop tank, front view – note relationship of pylon to ejector housing on top of the wing

SURA Rockets - post-mounted

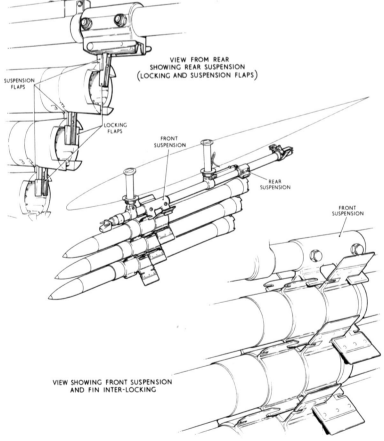

VIEW FROM REAR
SHOWING REAR SUSPENSION
(LOCKING AND SUSPENSION FLAPS)

SUSPENSION
FLAPS

LOCKING
FLAPS

FRONT
SUSPENSION

REAR
SUSPENSION

FRONT
SUSPENSION

VIEW SHOWING FRONT SUSPENSION
AND FIN INTER-LOCKING

F.58 nose showing the lumps for the ECM equipment

F.58 tail bullet, with ECM equipment housings

The same pylon with a small multiple ejector rack attached

Close-up of the flare dispenser unit

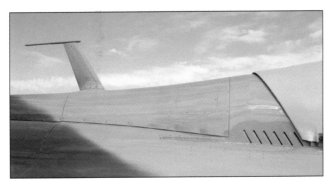

VHF aerial on the spine behind the cockpit

F.58 extended link collector tanks with flare dispensers

IFF aerial on the undersides, just aft of the nosewheel bay

Swiss Hunters carried an extra pylon inboard of the standard inner pylon

Unit badge for Swiss 5ieme Escadrille

Modelling the Hunter

Hunter kits are now available in all the major scales and here I present a selection of build reports and conversions covering each of these; I have tried to use some aftermarket details and decals with each build, though this is not always necessary. I have built many of these kits from the 'average' modeller's viewpoint; where possible, I have highlighted errors and suggested corrections, but with some kits, especially the older moulds, this task can be seriously intimidating. More capable modellers will no doubt have their own methods and suggestions and it's always worthwhile seeking their advice.

Main undercarriage in 1/32

Revell 1/32 Hunter FGA.9
Kit No. RG 4703

This kit was the bee's knees back in 1998 when it was first released, as there really wasn't a good IM Hunter kit available at that time. Producing the Hunter in this scale must have been a leap of faith for Revell, given the fact that the type was not operated by either the German or US armed forces, combined with being in a larger and (then) less popular scale. Having said that, they have since released the kit in its F.6 form, so the interest must still be there, and we can only hope that, having released lovely kits of the Hunter in 1/144 and 1/72 kits as well, Revell will choose to produce a worthy 1/48 kit to complete the quartet!

Back to this kit, and one is struck by the size of the box, with its well rendered artwork. Removing the lid, one finds the box

True Details 1/32 Hunter cockpit

chock with sprues and a very large decal sheet. The instruction booklet contains pictorial diagrams, but no reference materials. Surface detail is finely-worked engraved lines and rivets and while the cockpit interior has adequate detail for the scale, I had decided to incorporate the reasonably-priced True Details resin set, so most of the kit detail was consigned to the spares box.

The kit's ejection seat represents a Martin-Baker Mk.3 and is made up of 6 pieces; though it doesn't capture all the intricacies of the real thing, you could add some scratchbuilt detail and a set of harnesses and it would provide a perfectly adequate seat if you don't wish to purchase an aftermarket item. The cockpit tub is a little shallow, but once again the detail is not bad – careful painting and dry-brushing, plus the judicious addition of some

scratchbuilt detail will give good results, and with the canopy closed it would look fine; similarly, the instrument panel is nice right out of the box.

The True Details resin cockpit detail set is partly-based on the kit parts, but has added depth and detail to the side consoles and a substantial improvement on the detail behind the seat. Speaking of the seat, True Details provides a highly-detailed Martin-Baker Mk.2H that will repay careful painting and shading; reference to the ejection seat photos in this book will help you get the most from this part. All I added was a green oxygen hose on the right side; this was made from a piece of fine wire coiled around a flexible copper wire core, then coated with white glue before being painted.

Filling out the cockpit are a fine instrument panel, a very well detailed control column and a very nice gunsight to mount on the console. In addition, True Details has created a pair of very fine cockpit sidewalls. This is an area that Revell have left blank, and the resin parts really add a new level of busyness to the completed cockpit. The sidewalls fit perfectly, but I needed to mark their position carefully with the tub in place to ensure this – their tops are level with the kit's canopy sill.

With the cockpit painted, I turned to fuselage construction. Each fuselage half is split into three parts; the forward fuselage is separated at the intake area, and there is a separate tailcone. This suggests that Revell were planning a new nose section for the trainer versions; the spine behind the cockpit is also a

separate part, as is the tailcone, so the important differences are covered. I understand that sales of this large scale model have been somewhat disappointing though, so the Hunter trainer may never see the light of day, though the recent Fisher Models conversion set alleviates this to some extent. In any case, I glued each nose section to its counterpart centre fuselage and tailcone. By carefully joining these parts, I avoided the possibility of misalignment of the nose and tail sections to the centre fuselage, saving some time filling and sanding.

Next up, I made up the intake trunking and compressor face assembly. Unlike their 1/144 and 1/72 cousins, these kits have a full intakes and trunking, allowing for a much more realistic look. This assembly is a tight squeeze into the now-one-piece fuselage halves, but a little fiddling ensures a tight fit before gluing the halves together.

Turning to the wings, Revell has moulded the wing leading edge extensions (the 'dog-teeth') as separate elements, which allows for an accurate under-camber to be built into these areas when the model is complete. The wingtips are also separate and not the best of fits – some fiddling is necessary here. The flaps are separate as well, though once again, these wouldn't normally be open on the ground – use 'modeller's licence' with caution!

The undercarriage is adequately detailed – though this is a relatively simple area in real life anyway. One area that could stand improvement is the mainwheel well, where some detail would add more life to this area. All the undercarriage doors fit well into their wells – just as well, as the serial decals need to be added over them.

The windscreen is a good fit, and the sliding canopy slots easily onto its rails. Each was masked and positioned with white glue prior to painting, as I wanted to have the canopy open on the finished model to show off all that lovely True Details resin.

Armament is limited to some drop tanks and a pair of Matra rocket pods; however, Revell kindly provide the Sura rocket hardpoints if you wish to add them – these were frequently seen on FGA.9s even when the aircraft wasn't carrying the rockets or the launch rails.

The decals are very comprehensive, featuring hundreds of stencils. Unfortunately, my sheet was very poor and most of the decals were unusable. I managed to salvage some of the stencilling with decal film, but I decided to use an Aeromaster

decal sheet for the main markings. Their sheet 32-001 features markings for XE622/A of 28 Squadron, based in Hong Kong during the early 1960s. This squadron used yellow wingtips, so I first painted the outer wings in white, then gave them a good coating with yellow. I masked off the areas I wished to stay yellow, then painted the main camouflage colours, including Aluminium on the undersides, as used on these aircraft until the late-sixties.

The model was completed by adding a couple of aerials and the pitot on the port wing. This was a pretty easy build considering the size of the model – parts breakdown is mostly logical and consistent, and there are no real hang-ups. It was a pity about my decals sheet, but I am hopeful that it was an isolated case as I haven't heard of others having this problem. Accuracy is very good, with the only issue being that the dogtooth is set about 2mm too far outboard –a common problem with Revell Hunters. Overall, this is a nice kit and an ideal introduction to larger 1/32 scale kits.

Revell 1/32 FGA.9 in 28 Squadron colours

The cockpit in place on the 1/32 FGA.9

ACADEMY HOBBY MODEL KITS   Academy 1/48 Hunter F.6
Kit No. 2164

Academy released two 1/48 Hunters, an F.6 and an FGA.9, back in the mid-eighties; these are beautiful kits, with very nice engraved detail and overall very good fit, but as Hunter models they are seriously deficient. Here's one I made some years ago,

incorporating the Aeroclub correction set. The base kit has some serious accuracy problems and Aeroclub's set is really a necessity if you wish to produce anything like an accurate model. Some of the more egregious errors are as follows:

• 1. The ejection seat is badly undersized, being closer to 1/60 scale, and is in critical need of replacement. Martin-Baker Mk.2 or Mk.3 seats are available from various manufacturers in resin or white metal – see Chapter 6 for details. I used the white metal one from the Aeroclub correction set – this also helps with nose weight – and added a set of tape seatbelts and overhead pull handles.

• 2. The cockpit tub is much too shallow and will need to be replaced also; Aeroclub provides a deeper, more detailed replacement, though it might be possible to modify the kit part.

• 3. The tailcone is incorrect for either mark. The F.6 one is much too small in diameter; the FGA.9's is also too small in diameter and the brake parachute housing is not bulky enough and too pointed at the rear. The Aeroclub set provides three new correct tailcones for the Avon 100-series F.1 to 4, and for the Avon 200-series F.6 and FGA.9, with the natural metal exhaust tip reproduced in white metal – when polished, this looks really nice.

• 4. The tailplanes should be positioned some 2.5mm further forward and the associated anti-buffet bullet shortened by 3 mm. It's easy to lengthen the slot in the fin, but you should also add the plate that serves to seal the gap between the fin and variable-incidence tailplane. The shape of the plate is already engraved on the fin; it should be slightly raised, so I traced the shapes onto 5 thou plastic card before cutting them out and gluing them to the fin.

To simulate the rear formation lamp housing, I added a piece of clear sprue then sanded it to a point. I trimmed about 2.5 mm from the front of the hole in the fin created by removing the bullet, in effect moving the bullet forward by that much, and thereby retaining its spatial relationship with the elevators. With the shortened and reshaped bullet firmly glued in place and blended in with filler, I was able to attach the tailplanes in their correct position. Simple really…

• 5. The one big construction issue is the fit of the intake assembly to the fuselage and wings. Academy's suggested sequence of construction is to attach the intake trunking to the fuselage halves and close them before adding the wings at a later stage. This causes all sorts of fit issues and has given much grief to many modellers. A far easier method is to construct the wings and firmly attach them to the fuselage halves first. There is minimal gluing surface for this and I used superglue to assure a firm join; other types of glue could be used to literally weld the parts together. Once completely set, you can dry-fit the intake

assembly into the fuselage, adjusting the fit by filing and sanding as necessary. The fit will be tight, but as long as you attached the wings firmly, you shouldn't get any cracking or splitting. Once you are ready to join the fuselage halves, attach the intake assembly to one half; I used tube cement for this to give some time to adjust the fit before it all set up once the fuselage halves have been joined. A word about the intake assembly – ensure this is also firmly glued together, as the process of dry-fitting may cause the seams to split. It should also be noted that the intake splitter plates included with the kit are much too thick, and sit too far from the intake walls. Given the way they've been moulded, these cannot reasonably be corrected so I replaced mine with a piece of 10 thou plastic card to which I added a slight curve to match the contours of the fuselage side. These are mounted slightly proud of the fuselage - the mounts were made from short pieces of fine rod.

• 6. The kit's mainwheel tyres are about a mm. small in diameter. The white metal ones include with Aeroclub's correction set are about a mm. too large, and it's your choice as to which you'd prefer to correct! I chose to carefully sand back the Aeroclub ones, but the kit ones could be modified with a strip of 10 thou plastic card cemented to the outside of the tread. A related issue is that the kit's undercarriage legs are slightly too long – Aeroclub supply white metal legs to replace these.

• 7. Some panel lines are in the wrong places. For example, the kit has trim tabs on each aileron, whereas there should only be one on the port wing – see the plans included with this book.

• 8. I replaced my canopy with the vacform one by Aeroclub. The kit's windscreen is OK, if a little thick, but the sliding canopy

The instrument panel

is not correctly shaped, having the bulge apex too far back, being too short, and having a prominent rear frame, something the real Hunter canopy does not have – there is a thin Perspex strip inside the rear edge of the canopy that aids with a pneumatic pressurization strip.

I finished my model with the kit's decals for XE597 of 63 Squadron, based at Waterbeach in 1958. The other option in the kit is for an aircraft of 65 Squadron. XE597 was that used by 63 Squadron's commanding officer, Sqn Ldr Walker, and featured a colourful black and yellow checked fin and tailplanes, reflecting the squadron's colours. The special markings were applied shortly before the squadron disbanded. These are applied as large decals, and line up quite well, with minimal touch-up required on the leading edge.

RAF Hunters had their underside serial numbers straddling the undercarriage doors, which makes for awkward application for the modeller; the real things were painted with the aircraft

on stands and the u/c up! While some decal manufacturers add helpful cutting lines that divide each serial into the parts of each door, others don't. The easiest way to deal with this is to temporarily attach the undercarriage doors to the wings; I use poster putty for this, but using white glue to tack-glue them in place also works. With these in place, I attach the decals and allow them to dry thoroughly. Then using a new scalpel blade, I carefully cut along the edges of the doors, slicing the decals. It's then a simple matter to remove the doors, seal in the decals with Future and set them aside for final assembly.

While this seems a lot of work, in the end this is currently the best way to get an accurate 1/48 scale Hunter.

The intake trunking in place, firmly secured with superglue

The Aeroclub cockpit

The indifferent fit of PJ's replacement nose undertray

Academy 1/48 Hunter F.6 Conversion to GA.11
Kit No. 2164

Philippe Jacques of PJ Production kindly sent me a sample of his 1/48 Hunter GA.11 resin conversion set, and so I purchased another Academy F.6 kit, although the FGA.9 kit would also be suitable – the kits are the same aside from the tailcone, which for this conversion is replaced by an Aeroclub part as will be related. Of course, the decals from either kit will be inappropriate, and I purchased the Model Alliance sheet 48-136, which has two options for the GA.11, one with and one without the Harley Light in the nose. I opted for the FRADU Hunter with the Harley Light, XE685/'861', in the overall Dark Sea Grey scheme of the early 1980s.

The same basic issues with the Academy parts need to be addressed, and I used a combination of parts from Aeroclub and

PJ Production to correct these. The PJ set comprises a new cockpit tub, Martin-Baker Mk.3 seat and instrument panel for the cockpit; a new lower nose piece without gun troughs to replace the kit part; a clear resin nose to represent the Harley Light; an arrestor hook; and sundry small items. It doesn't include a new tailcone and so you'll have to either purchase an Aeroclub set or work on enlarging the kit parts.

The PJ resin seat is very nice indeed, with a representation of both sets of belts. The PJ cockpit tub is nicely detailed and the correct depth, and the new seat fits nicely into this.

As the GA.11 airframe was based on the F.4 fuselage, I used the appropriate tailcone pieces from Aeroclub's set. Interestingly, the kit's 'F.6' tailcone is so narrow that it easily slides into the correct Aeroclub F.4 pieces! Aeroclub also supply a nice white metal ring. The GA.11 was gunless, so PJ provides a new lower nose piece to directly replace the kit parts that have the gun troughs. Unfortunately, due to shrinkage this part is too small, being too short and too shallow. You could use plastic card as shims, but I elected to use the kit part and filled in the troughs. Being gunless, you should not fit the cartridge link collector tanks ('Sabrinas'), nor the gunsight which was removed from FRADU aircraft.

PJ also provides a solid, clear resin nosecone to replace the kit part, to represent the Harley Light. After studying photos, I decided that this part gives too large a diameter to the light, and doesn't incorporate enough of a lip/rim in front of the lens cover. In addition, there is no representation of the lens behind the cover, which doesn't look very convincing. I elected to use the kit nose, and carefully cut off the extreme tip 1mm in front of the first panel line. Using a sharp curved scalpel blade, I carefully shaped a new lip. I had a 6.4mm diameter MV Lenses clear lens that I positioned inside the nose cone, just behind the lip. This looks just right and gives a better impression of depth to this important feature on the GA.11. After adding nose weight, I secured the nose cone to the fuselage.

Assembly proceeded in the same manner as my previous Academy Hunter build. I added the new airfield arrestor hook, then carefully positioned the tail bumper slightly to port to clear the hook. I added the two 100-gallon drop tanks, though FRADU Hunters were often seen with four – two others would have to be sourced from elsewhere, however. GA.11s were never fitted for the larger 230-gallon tanks, nor did the flaps include the cut-out to accommodate these – you will need to fill in the panel line that represents this.

From 1984, FRADU Hunters were painted overall glossy Dark Sea Grey (DSG) and this was the scheme I opted to represent. After pre-shading the panel lines, Xtracrylix paint was used for the DSG; I used two coats and buffed out the paint after both to give a deeper and more realistic sheen. Decals were from Model Alliance sheet 48-136, which has two options for the GA.11, one being XE685/'861'.

My preferred method of applying decals is as follows: firstly, I soak the decal in very warm water – this better softens the decal than lukewarm or cold water, and is also quicker. While it is soaking, I add a small patch of Future to the location where the decal will sit. While this is wet, I apply the decal over the top, ensuring it is correctly positioned. When I am happy with the location, I use a cotton bud to wick away excess Future. Any drying marks left by the Future can be easily removed with a water-dampened cotton bud. When the decals and Future are thoroughly dry, I add a top coat of Future to seal them in. Using this method, I rarely have issues with silvering, which was often a problem for me using setting solutions. As always with a new method, try it out on an old model first.

Turning now to the undercarriage, I replaced the kit's wheels and legs with replacement parts by Aeroclub. The kit's wheels are all slightly too small, and in compensation, the legs are slightly too long. These can be corrected fairly easily, if one desires, by adding a strip of 10 thou plastic card around the tread of the tyres, and by shortening the legs by about 2 mm. This greatly improves the sit of the model. As I had the white metal parts available, I opted to use them and these require a bit of cleanup, especially the mainwheels. These require about a mm to be removed from the tread to bring them down to the correct diameter.

I added a couple of aerials on each side of the lower nose – these were associated with the TACAN aerial navigation equipment fitted to these aircraft in the vacant gunbays. The last item added was the pitot tube on the port wing.

This was an interesting build, and results in an appealing model of a type from the tail end of the Hunter's career.

PJ Production 1/72 Hawker Hunter F.6/FGA.9/FR.10/FGA.57
Kit No. 721022

This is a resin kit, with white metal and etched brass parts. There are four variants offered; parts and markings are included for the following aircraft:

- F.6 of 325 Sqn, RNethAF, late 1950s
- FGA.9 of 8/42 Sqn, Aden, 1966
- FR.10 (or more properly FR.71A) of 8 Grupo, Chilean Air Force, 1976
- FGA.57 of Kuwaiti Air Force, late 1960s

Included are all the appropriate substitute parts for the 4 versions. Therefore, there are alternate fin/rudders, tail sections with and without braking parachute housing, ejection seats and noses. For the FR.10, the camera nose is molded in clear resin. The resin is cleanly molded with no warping and few air bubbles.

I had decided to build the Dutch F.6, although a quick dry fit suggests that all the alternate parts would fit equally well. I was able to use many parts from this kit for conversions – see elsewhere in this chapter. With that in mind, I first studied the clear and concise instruction sheet and set aside all unneeded parts. All parts were thoroughly scrubbed clean of any release agents.

Construction commences with the nicely detailed cockpit. The tub is cast integrally with the nosewheel bay; both areas were appropriately painted and weathered before installation into the starboard fuselage half. There is some sidewall detail and aligning the tub is easy. Into the tub is inserted the Martin-Baker Mk.2 ejection seat, which is appropriate for this version. The overhead pull handle is cast separately – this aids with painting and alleviates possible breakage of this very delicate part. The instrument panel is molded with its shroud and this also features good detail. This part is firmly attached to recesses in the top of the tub sidewalls. All in all, assembly here presents no difficulties. I had pre-painted both the instrument panel and seat in 'Interior Black' (Or very, very dark grey if you prefer!) with other colors picked out as necessary. Don't forget to add some nose weight before closing the fuselage halves.

The fuselage halves fit well after cleaning up, but one thing I hadn't noticed on my first inspection was that some of the under fuselage panel lines do not match up very well at the seam. I tidied them up a little, but didn't do much in the way of re-

PJ Production 1/72 F.6 in Dutch 325 Squadron markings

PJ Production 1/72 GA.11
(F.6/F/4 hybrid – see text!)

scribing – the top fuselage panel lines line up perfectly, by the way. The nose is a separate piece to accommodate different versions. Be sure to thoroughly clean up the pour stub, as the back of the nosepiece can be seen as the front wall of the nosewheel bay. No filler was needed after attachment, as not only does the part fit very well, the seam is a natural panel line.

Each wing is moulded in one piece; after clean-up these fit very well to the fuselage with just a smidgeon of filler required to blend them in. Neither the fuselage halves nor the wings were warped to even the slightest degree. The wings feature full undercarriage bays, though due to the thickness of the resin these are a little shallow. The engine intakes feature full trunking with nice contouring, except that where the wing meets the fuselage there is just a blank wall. I painted these areas of the fuselage black so that it is less noticeable, but the more dedicated may wish to open up sections of the fuselage to show the front engine fan and accessory compartment.

The rear fuselage insert fits well along a panel line, with just a little filler needed to blend it in. Once this is dry, the vertical tail fits neatly into a slot in the fuselage and in turn, each horizontal tailplane slots to this, though you will probably have to trim the tabs a bit as I did.

With the basic airframe complete, it was time to paint and decal. PJ provides a useful painting guide with callouts in the correct color names rather than by reference to a particular paint company. I used Xtracrylix Dark Green and Dark Sea Grey over Testors Metalizer Dull Aluminium. Once coated with Future, the glossy surface provided a fine surface for decals.

PJ's decals are top quality for the most part. Thin yet strong, they pulled down into panel line detail while I watched, but are dense enough to fully cover changes in paint colour. Absolutely no solvents or setting solutions were used or necessary and no silvering occurred even with the smallest stencils. The only problem I noticed was a slight misregistration of the white that really showed on the Dutch unit badge and on a couple of the stencils. A quick lick of camouflage paint put this to rights, but otherwise these are splendid decals.

Attention turns to the fiddly bits, and there are some good ones in this kit. PJ offers a fully detailed ventral airbrake; however, this was rarely deployed on the ground as due to low clearance, the airbrake was automatically closed when the undercarriage was deployed for landing and remained inoperable until the landing gear was retracted after take-off. I

decided to fit it slightly open as if there had been a drop in hydraulic pressure – something you can occasionally see in photos of the Hunter.

Similarly, it is rare to see the flaps extended on the ground, particularly on RAF Hunters as pilots took care to retract these after landing to prevent any damage, either to the aircraft or their wallets; it is a tradition that pilots who forget to do this are fined a round at the Squadron Mess. However, looking at many photos of export Hunters, it seems that many foreign air forces do not have this tradition, so I felt justified in dropping the flaps on my Dutch Hunter, and so was able to use the excellent etched brass pieces that PJ include! Each flap has only three cleverly designed pieces, but care is needed to get them just right.

The undercarriage is provided as white metal castings. These don't have quite the sharpness of detail as the resin parts, but are necessary to carry the weight of the resin castings. The scissor links on the main u/c are etched brass. The undercarriage bay doors are all in resin and are a bit fragile – two of mine had broken in transit. The only missing detail here are the jacks that attach the rear nosewheel bay door to the nosewheel leg to pull it closed on retraction. I added these with fine wire, as they are very noticeable in photos.

The only stores provided are 100 and 230-gallon drop tanks, so those who wish to build the FGA.9 with armament will need to raid their spares box. As the Dutch were one of only 3 countries to wire their Hunters for Sidewinders, I decided to add a Sidewinder shoe and missile from my spares box to each outer wing pylon.

PJ provides two duplicate vacform canopies, always a good idea as far as I am concerned! The clarity of these left a little to be desired, as there were a few blemishes, perhaps from improperly cleaned masters? A coat of Future helped to hide these and restored clarity after sanding and trimming. It was relatively easy to detach the canopies from their sheet, as the frames are quite obvious. Trimming to fit was a different matter, as the canopy is a touch wider than the cockpit, so I got the best fit I could and attached it to the model with white glue. A nice final touch is an etched brass ladder, though there is no indication on the instructions as to where to attach this. And with that, the model is finished.

There is no doubt that this is a fine little kit. There are no pitfalls in construction and the only other criticism I have is that the kit doesn't include any armament. While this is a nice package and simply a pleasure to build – is ideal as a first resin kit – the dimensional shortfall will be an issue to some.

PJ Production 1/72 F.6 Diables Rouge Conversion to GA.11
Kit No. 721013

This kit is basically similar to the kit reviewed above, but can be made up to represent a Belgian Air Force Diables Rouge aircraft. I decided to convert it to a Royal Navy GA.11. This was a relatively simple job, given that the kit had an F.4 fuselage and F.6 wings – I am assured by Philippe that this was an issue in the initial run of this kit, but was corrected in subsequent batches. Having said that, this was fortunate for me, as changing or modifying the tailcone would have been interesting! As a result, this left me with the relatively simple tasks of removing all traces of the cannon troughs and adding an airfield arrestor hook. As I was also building a GA.11 in 1/48 with a Harley Light nose, I decided to leave the earlier standard nose on this model.

The simple but elegant Extra Dark Sea Grey over White colour scheme common to 1960s Fleet Air Arm aircraft was chosen, and markings were found on Model Art decal sheet 72-056. Three options are offered and I chose to use those for an aircraft of the Rough Diamonds aerobatic team, 738 NAS based at Brawdy in 1965. The standard markings are supplemented by a white Pegasus on the nose. The decals worked well, but the white was rather translucent, and the red too bright, so I replaced the roundels with some from the spares box.

A pleasing build, and my happy accident in getting a kit with the incorrect type of fuselage meant that this build was quite easy. PJ's kits are quite straightforward and are ideal first resin kits. While the F.6 kits have been discontinued, the F.4 and F.4/5 kits (721014 and -15, respectively) are still available at the time of writing.

FROG Frog 1/72 Hunter FGA.9
Kit No. 204

Frog's FGA.9 dates from 1972, and so exhibits little in the way of detail and has fine raised panel lines. However, with a bit of work, it is a reasonable starting point for a nice little model. In this case, I decided to use parts left over from the PJ Production Hunter kit, reviewed above, to convert the Frog kit to an RAF FR.10 recce plane. These included a new tail, tail cone, nose with camera ports and drop tanks.

There are 46 parts in the Frog kit, including a reasonable single-piece canopy. Also in the box are an adequate instruction sheet with exploded diagrams, and a small decal sheet with two options.

Compared to photos and plans, I found that the rear fuselage is a little fat, by about 1-2mm; the nose is slightly short and skinny; and the outer wings are too broad. Also, the cockpit is set too low on the fuselage, giving a slightly flat look that would be difficult to correct.

To start correcting some of these problems, I was able to sand back the outer wings to a more accurate shape starting from the dogtooth, noting that the angle of sweepback should be greater than for the inner wing, rather than the same as depicted on the kit parts. Also of note is that the dogtooth is located about 2 mm too far outboard, though I wasn't going to fret about it for this build. The nose problem would be taken care of with the PJ leftover part. With this in mind, I cut off the nose at the forward edge of the nosewheel bay. I also removed the fin, as the spare resin part was more to scale thickness, and the rear fuselage at the tail cone attachment point to accommodate the new tail cone.

Inside the fuselage, I made a number of additions. For the cockpit, the kit offers only a basic seat and floor, so some detailing was called for. From plastic card I added a front undercarriage bay roof, and front and rear cockpit bulkheads. Between these was positioned a cockpit floor to which sidewalls were attached. None of these was heavily detailed, as the dark interior and closed canopy wouldn't allow much to be seen. I used the spare PJ MB 3 ejection seat. A control column and an instrument panel from the spares box rounded out the interior. Don't forget to add some nose weight – I used two small fishing weights for this. The kit's nose is a little too narrow, so I shimmed it with 10 thou plastic card to match the width of the resin nose. This was then attached and faired in with small dabs of filler. The cannon troughs are very crude, and I decided to open these out a bit using my rotary tool. A few FR.10s had their cannon ports faired over so this isn't strictly necessary, but a photo of your chosen aircraft would be helpful.

Mating the tail cone to the fuselage showed that Frog's fuselage is about 2 mm wider at this point than PJ's, so I set about sanding down the rear fuselage until less portly

Frog 1/72 FGA.9 converted to FR.10

Revell 1/72 F.6 with Modeldecal markings for No.1 Squadron

dimensions were achieved. This meant having to add a layer of superglue inside the end of the rear fuselage, as sanding down the plastic to match the resin ended with a wafer-thin layer of Frog's original material remaining. The parts were then blended together with filler.

The Frog parts feature fine raised panel lines, many of which were lost in the conversion and those remaining were sanded down – in this scale, I only rescribed the most important of these. I also opened out various intakes and openings in the airframe. The ventral airbrake is molded shut, but as Hunters generally have these closed on the ground, this was not important. The main engine intakes are very crude and I elected to conceal them with simple intake covers.

The fit of the Frog parts is generally good with just a little filler required at the wing/fuselage joins. Blending in the new PJ fin was a little more problematic, as it is much thinner than the kit fin. I added a strip of 20 thou to each side of the fin's locating tab and this filled most of the gap left by removing the old fin. Some blending with filler evened out the remaining roughness in this area. The kit's tailplanes slot into the PJ fin with a little trimming; I also thinned these down somewhat to blend better with the new fin.

The kit's decals offer options for Swiss AF and RAF machines. For my 1964 RAF FR.10 the color scheme is Dark Green and Dark Sea Grey over High Speed Silver; I used decals from Modeldecal sheet number 86 that depict an aircraft of 4 Sqn, RAF Germany.

Once painting and decalling were complete, it was time to add the fiddly bits. The undercarriage parts are pretty good considering their vintage. The undercarriage bays are too shallow and are completely lacking in detail, but I confined my efforts to simply blanking off the sides and adding a little structure and pipework.

The kit's rocket pods and drop tanks are poorly detailed and were discarded, but luckily the drop tanks from the PJ kit were still available. FR.10s really didn't carry any other external stores, and a full load of 100- and 230-gallon drop tanks is appropriate. The final touch is the canopy, which is not too bad, though the frames are a little heavy. It sits a bit low on the fuselage, like it is hunched up a bit, but there is not much that can be done about this short of major surgery.

So there we have it - but was it worth it? The process was fairly enjoyable, and I have a nice looking (if a little chubby)

recce Hunter. With both the PJ and Revell kits on the market, the Frog Hunter can in all honesty be assigned to the collector's realm. Although it was not bad for its day, sadly that day has now passed. But if you enjoy a little nostalgia, then this is a good kit to get a generous helping!

Revell 1/72 Hawker Hunter F.6
Kit No. 04350

When the Revell F.6 was released in 2005, it was the first all-new 1/72 injection molded Hunter for nigh-on 30 years, and received a warm welcome from builders of classic jets. The kit is molded in light grey plastic and the parts are finely detailed with engraved lines and some areas of rivets, all of which are delicate and scale appropriate. The breakdown of the parts would allow Revell to release all earlier and later marks of the Hunter in the future, though a two-seater would require a new fuselage mold. The tail cone and wing leading edges included in this kit are appropriate for the F.6 and derived versions.

Cockpit detail is nice, with a four-piece seat to fit in a tub that includes side panels, and a finely detailed instrument panel. A separate nose cone points to other variants. The undercarriage is also nicely detailed and fits agreeably into the equally nicely detailed wheel wells. Separate flaps and air brake are included, though once again for RAF aircraft, these would normally be raised while the aircraft was on the ground.

Stores provided are limited to drop tanks, though two Sidewinders are provided for the Dutch option. Again, it's a pity that rocket pods or bombs were not included. The canopy is in two parts and the sliding section fits nicely over the fuselage if posed open.

Construction is relatively pain-free, though I was concerned about the wing construction which I feel to be overly complicated. To accommodate the 'dog-tooth' leading edge of later mark Hunters, the outer leading edges are separate parts, but for some reason Revell have also included the wingtips as separate parts as well. This wouldn't be a problem if they all fit well, but both pairs of parts are a little thicker than the main wing structure, leading to a sanding job that erases some of that fine engraved detail.

Another problem with the kit is the wing-fuselage join, which leaves a bit of a step where there should be a smooth transition – some delicate work with a sanding stick and a little filler will alleviate this, but I would not have expected this problem in a modern kit. Finally, although the intake splitter plates are included - a first for this scale - the curved intake trunks are not represented at all, leaving a yawning hole in each wing. One can either create intake trunks with thin plastic card, or use putty to mold the shape inside the wing. Or you could opt out and add intake covers! But again, this is something one would not expect in a modern kit. Nor is the fact that when the wings are fitted, there are large gaps to fill inside the intakes at both the top and bottom edges.

Having got these gripes out of the way, I have to say that this is otherwise an excellent kit. Construction is easy, fit otherwise is excellent, no other filler is required and detail is extremely nice. Checking against plans and photos, the completed model looks very fine, the only minor issue being that the dog-tooth is about 1mm further outboard than it should be.

Four decal options are included, two RAF, one Belgian and one Dutch. These are:
- 1. F.6 XG204, Fighter Combat School, RAF, 1961
- 2. F.6 XF462, 66Sqn RAD, 1959
- 3. F.6 N-283, 324 Sqn RNethAF, 1957
- 4. F.6 IF-126/IS-U, 22 Sqn Belgian AF, 1960

The aftermarket has provided lots more options; as the RAF alone had 21 F.6 squadrons, the sky's the limit! I opted to use Modeldecal markings for 1 Sqn, but used the kit stencils and national markings. These went down well, although the roundel white was a little translucent.

Overall this is a nice kit that, even with the minor problems I have pointed out, is far superior to any other injection moulded Hunter in this scale.

Matchbox 1/72 Hawker Hunter T.7/FGA.9
Kit No. PK-116

Not currently in any catalogues, but still readily available second-hand, Matchbox's T.7 is the only two-seat Hunter kit in this scale, although Revell may release one in future; PJ's resin conversion, detailed below, is the only other way to model a T-bird. Released in 1976, the kit has parts for both the FGA.9

single-seater and two-seat T.7, particularly separate nose sections, and comes on three sprues molded in dark and medium blue – yuck! In this boxing, decals are included for an RAF T.7 from 45 Squadron in the mid-seventies, though later boxings included decals for the 92 Sqn Blue Diamonds trainer, or one from 1417 Flight in Oman.

Surface detail is of the coarse engraved trenches that so endeared Matchbox to our hearts. These were filled and sanded smooth, with the most important panel lines restored by lightly engraving.

Interior detail is typical Matchbox – virtually non-existent! I scratchbuilt a basic cockpit tub with side consoles and added a pair of suitable white metal ejection seats, then used the instrument panel decal included on the decal sheet to make a plastic card instrument panel. As it is all basically black, not much detail can be seen through a closed canopy so I really didn't go to town here. Nose weight was added to prevent tail-sitting. I attached each nose section half to their respective fuselage halves; this helps to lessen the mismatch, though much filler is still needed to blend them together.

Before attaching the wings to the fuselage, I needed to modify the outer wings, as these are much too broad from the dogtooth outwards. Starting at the tip by removing 4mm and tailing off to meet the dogtooth, plastic needs to be removed from the leading edge to create a sharper angle. The tips themselves also need to be reshaped. While not perfect, the wings do look a lot better for this. I added plastic card to box in the wheel wells and some strip to add some basic detail, and also added intake trunks from Tamiya two-part putty, which I smoothed to give a nice curved appearance. If you don't do this, you'll be able to see the undercarriage through the intakes – not very realistic!

Fit of the parts is poor throughout and a lot of filler was required to get a smooth finish for the glossy paint scheme. The biggest outline fault of the kit is the nose, which is inaccurate in shape and slightly too long. I added putty to the inside of the nose area, along with some nose weight, before joining the fuselage halves together. The nose was then drastically sanded down, shaving about 2mm from the length, while reshaping the tip of the nose, and adding more curvature to the top decking forward of the windscreen. This makes things look a lot better,

Matchbox 1/72 T.7 in 45 Squadron markings

though it's not perfect by any means – the nose does not narrow enough towards the tip in plan view, and it would take a lot of work to bring this to an acceptable standard. Some years ago, I had purchased one of the old Air Conversions resin nose jobs, but after studying lots of photos I felt this was too short and not deep enough.

Other mods included beefing up the brake chute housing above the exhaust with putty, while creating an upsweep of the lower tail cone to better represent the back end of an Avon 100-series Hunter.

The decals were straight from the box, with the addition of some spare Revell stencilling. Matchbox provides decals for a T.7 of 45 Squadron based at RAF Wittering in 1974. They are very basic, but adequately printed and just about usable. The roundels had a sliver of white bordering one side, which was

Opening up the engine intakes of the Revell 1/72 kit...

...and creating the intake trunking with filler

over-painted with the correct camouflage colours once dry.

The model was completed by adding the undercarriage and pylons. Overall, this was an interesting project – simple, but time-consuming given the amount of filler needed, and in reshaping the nose. It's your typical Matchbox kit – it needs work! With the release of the PJ Production conversion set for the Revell kit, the Matchbox kit can be considered redundant, but if you have one in your stash and are prepared to do some major rhinoplasty, a passable T.7 can be added to your collection of Hunter models.

PJ Production 1/72 Hunter T.7 Conversion Set
Kit No. 721207 (Applied to Revell FGA.9)

While the Hunter modeller has had it pretty good in recent years, with the excellent Revell F.6 and FGA.9 kits in 1/144, 1/72 and 1/32, the poor T-bird has been rather neglected; luckily, Aeroclub (1/48), Fisher Models (1/32) and Philippe Jacques of PJ Production in Belgium have come to our rescue with resin conversion sets in all three major scales that enables the modeller to create almost any Hunter two-seater. PJ has chosen the Revell 1/72 kit as the donor for his set.

Philippe was kind enough to send me a test shot of this new set, which is intended for either of the Revell kits, though you should take note that not all T-bird variants can be made using the F.6 kit – more on that later. Presented in PJ's usual blue box, there are a total of 22 pieces, some of which are optional; plus two vacformed canopies, there being a spare. The resin in this test shot was perfectly cast and features fine engraved panel lines where needed. Instructions are on four sides of paper with comprehensive instructions and colour drawings for the four aircraft included on the decal sheet (Not ready for inclusion with this test shot.).

The four options are:
- RAF – T.7, XL600/83 of 16 Sqn, January 1981
- Royal Navy – T.8, XL580 of Flag Office Flight Training, RNAS Yeovilton, 1960's
- Dutch Air Force – T.7, N-316, unknown unit, 1960s

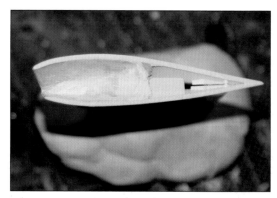

• Swiss AF – T.68, J-4203 of Fliegerstaffel 24, 1990. Includes
civil registration HB-RVM for post-military airshow career.

The nose section is the focus of this set, and PJ has included
vertically-split hollow-moulded nose halves. There are three
nose halves included – a standard starboard side and two
alternative port sides, one with and one without a cannon
fairing. This allows the modeller to build a either a single-gun
T.7/8 or a two-cannon export T-bird. The insides of these nose
halves feature recesses to align the cockpit tub. The tub is
moulded in one piece, complete with sidewalls and the central
console between the pilots, and there is some instrumentation
detail on these areas. The frontwheel well is moulded to the
underside of the tub, which gives very positive location for both
the tub and well.

Two Martin Baker MB.4 seats are included, and are nicely
detailed with complete belts. The instrument panel is moulded
integrally with the coaming, and this is a good representation of
the T.7 panel. Rather than painting it, I used a decal panel from
an old Modeldecal sheet I had available. The control columns are
nice; all parts were then fitted to the tub and given a light
drybrushing to bring out the detail.

Each nose half has a recessed area for the tub to rest into,
similarly for the frontwheel well, so there will be no issues with
alignment with these parts. With the tub in place, I added a

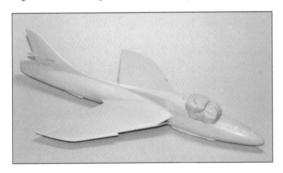

couple of fishing weights to the voids around it, just to prevent
any possibility of tail-sitting. The cockpit halves were superglued
together and these fit perfectly with a minimum of filler
required. Of note, these parts feature alignment pins, the first
time I have seen this on resin aftermarket parts and a very
helpful feature. With the cockpit halves together, I added the
nose cone – this being a separate piece to accommodate the
optional Swiss T.68, which had ECM lumps; an appropriately-
festooned piece is provided as an alternate.

With assembly of the new nose section completed, it was time
to irrevocably commit and do some surgery on the donor kit.
PJ's instructions tell you to remove the nose on a panel line just
inside the intakes – to allow for errors, I cut slightly ahead of
this line, then was able to sand back later.

One of the few shortcomings of the Revell Hunter is the
complete lack of intake detail. To me, this seriously compromises
the model, as it spoils the looks from ahead. However, I have a

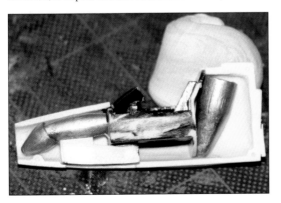

relatively easy fix that I have used on both my Revell builds.
There are two stages to this; firstly, creating the intake trunking,
which involves the wing assembly and secondly, creating a
representation of the Avon's first compressor face.

Taking the wings first, I glued the halves together, and then
spread a thin layer of putty to the roof and floor of the intake –
this prevents the possibility of a chemical reaction attacking the
plastic, as can happen if too thick a layer of putty is layered at
once. Once that had dried, I added a lump of putty into each
intake and using a damp cotton bud, I moulded this out to a
smooth curving surface, blending into both the floor and roof of
the trunk, extending forward to the intake lips and backwards to
the front of the wheel well wall. The aim is to get a smooth,
seamless transition from the intake lips to the side of the
fuselage. Once this is dry, it can be painted a dirty white, the
most common colour for Hunter intake trunking.

The second phase of this fix is to create a representation of
the front of the engine. Although this will be scarcely visible on
the completed model, it does add considerably to the realism
should someone stick a penlight into your Hunter's nostrils, as it
were! On each fuselage half, there is a recess where the wings fit
– some of this will be cut away. Just behind the L-shaped tabs
that hold the rear end of the intake splitter plate in place, I
marked a D-shape with a marker pen. Using a pin vice with a
No.65 drill bit, I chain drilled around this 'D', then once the
rough opening had been made, I smoothed things out with a
sharp knife blade, and a rat-tail file. On the inside of the
starboard fuselage, just behind the opening, I added a short tab
of plastic card, to which was glued a compressor face that was in
my spares box. Most engines of the era were pretty much the
same diameter and exact detail is not important, so anything
that looks remotely right will do – I think mine came from an
old Airfix Phantom! It needed a little sanding to get it to fit, but
the effect is just right.

With this stage done, I dry fit the wings to check on the fit of
my newly-created intake trunking. A little adjustment both ways
and a smooth transition can be made before gluing the wings
firmly into place. Before that happens though, it is best to attach
the nose section.

Mating the new nose to the fuselage showed an almost
perfect fit – the remnant pour stubs for the nose halves are
perfectly shaped to insert into the truncated Revell fuselage. Just
a smidgeon of filler was required to blend the two, and the panel
line was restored later in the build.

With the nose firmly in place, and the wings also attached,
the last large lump of resin to affix is the aft canopy fairing and
forward spine. Part of the kit's spine will need to be removed,
and this is clearly marked on the instruction sheet. Once again, I
cut a little ahead of the advised cut line so I could sand back for

The underside, waiting to cut
the serial decals and remove
the u/c bay doors

All primed and ready to go –
the clean conversion

PJ's hollow-cast nose halves
leave plenty of room for nose
weight

Frog FGA.9 converted to Swiss F.58 with PJ Production parts

an exact fit – and it does! I did have to use a little filler to blend the front into the back of the cockpit section, but that was entirely my fault – a little overzealous and uneven sanding of the pour stub at the front of the spine.

I have to say that the quality of the castings is very good with this set – the parts fit very well, and they are all cast very cleanly with thought given to the size and shape of the pour stubs.

Turning to the back end, there is a choice for the modeller, depending on the variant they wish to model, and this also affects the donor kit that the modeller will need to acquire. If the modeller wishes to build a two-seater with an Avon 200 engine – mostly export aircraft – then the tail cone included in the FGA.9 kit will be needed as this has the necessary brake parachute housing already moulded in place – this part is not included in the F.6 kit. Should the modeller wish to build an Avon 100-equipped T-bird – the RAF's T.7 and RN T.8s being the obvious ones here - then either the F.6 or FGA.9 kit can be used. In this case, the kit's tailcone is replaced by a very nice resin tailcone that accurately features the smaller diameter tailcone of the Avon 100, with the brake parachute housing that featured on all two-seat Hunters.

The new tailcone is an excellent fit, needing just a dab of filler to blend it in place. The forward fairings for the brake parachute housing are provided in very thin resin, but these needed some trimming to get them to fit properly. One aspect of the Avon 100 series that this set does not address is the slightly different configurations of the vents on the rear fuselage – I did not make any corrections on this model, but you may wish to refer to the photos in the walkaround section if you are so inclined.

The canopy I received with the test shot was not the final version, which was just as well as it did not fit particularly well! After much frustration and a botched attempt at fairing it in, I elected to separate the windscreen and canopy and pose it open. I had to do a lot of trimming to get the windscreen to fit, but the end result isn't too bad – considering my general ham-fistedness when it comes to vacform canopies! I added a piece of red-painted plastic rod to represent the canopy support strut that can often be seen in photos of two-seaters on the ground. I am assured by Philippe that the canopy for the production sets will

be better fitting!

With the airframe complete, I gave the model a good scrub, then a coat of primer. The inevitable clean-up of blemishes was acute this time, as I had elected to depict one of the High Speed Silver T-birds that graced a frontline fighter unit – in this case, 74 'Tiger' Squadron – and I wanted as smooth a finish as possible. Once I was satisfied, I gave the model a final primer coat and a light polishing.

Actual painting began with some Golden Yellow on the wings and just forward of the tail – these were masked off prior to overpainting. Over this, I gave the model two coats of Testors Metalizer Non-Buffing Aluminum, which give a durable and not too shiny finish which looks just right in this scale. The masking was removed and the model was given a coat of Future prior to decalling.

The 74 Squadron aircraft that I had chosen, XL620, is not one of the offered decal options – the decals were still at the printers when I received this sample – but it was easy enough to find the required decals in my spares box; some Modeldecal numbers and letters (still useful after all these years!), Xtradecal roundels and some homemade decals for the squadron's tiger head and tiger stripes on the nose. Note that '620 is one of the few regular service Hunters to appear with a sloped fin flash. Once applied, the decals were sealed in with another coat of Future.

The undercarriage was straight from the box, the nose leg fitting nicely into the new nose bay, while I added a single set of pylons and 100-gallon drop tanks under the wings. The final addition was the port wing pitot tube.

This is a very good set: easy to use and well-fitting, aside from the non-production canopy. Although I didn't have the production decals, the options are nice and having used PJ decals in the past, I would anticipate that they will be very easy to use. This set would make an ideal first conversion – the donor kit is excellent and the engineering of the conversion makes it child's play. The result is one of the most aesthetically-pleasing trainers ever, and a great addition to the display case.

PJ Production 1/72 Hawker Hunter F.58 Conversion
Kit No. 721202 (Applied to Frog FGA.9)

This conversion set is intended for the PJ kit reviewed earlier, and a quick dry fit revealed that the parts are cast such that they are straight replacements for the equivalent parts in the kit, making this a very easy conversion. However, I decided to see if this conversion would work with another kit; once again the venerable Frog Hunter FGA.9 was my guinea pig. Sometimes, this hobby makes you feel vaguely Dr. Frankenstein-ish.

The conversion contains the following parts relevant to the later Swiss F.58 modifications: replacement fin with ECM blisters on the rear bullet fairing, new drop tanks, enlarged spent cartridge collectors with chaff dispensers, new inner wing pylons, new nose cone with ECM blisters, and various other small bits. All these parts are cleanly cast with no obvious blemishes and incorporate good detail. The first step is to clean them thoroughly and remove them from their casting blocks, a quick and simple task. No decals are included, so I utilized those from the kit. Aftermarket decals for Swiss aircraft are also available from ModelArt and Cutting Edge.

To use the conversion, I cut off the Frog kit's fin at its base and the nose at the front of the nosewheel bay. Incorporating the resin parts to the kit was fairly simple. The kit's nose is a little too narrow, so I shimmed it with 10 thou to match the width of the resin nose and used a little filler to blend it all in. The resin fin's locating tab was also shimmed with 20 thou to make it the same width as the opening created by removing the kit fin, again blending in with filler. The kit spine ahead of the new fin also needed to be sanded to the new width. Of course, none of these actions would be necessary if using the conversion with the PJ Hunter kit.

In addition to changes in the Frog kit to incorporate the new resin parts, I corrected some errors and added some more detail, as outlined elsewhere in this chapter. Further additions for this mark that are not included with the conversion were the Maverick missiles plus pylon shoes, all sourced from my spares box. These were fitted to many Swiss machines from the mid-eighties. Sidewinders are another option, though you can't have both them and Mavericks at the same time!

The recent Revell Hunter FGA.9 kit includes all the relevant lumps and bumps for a Swiss F.58, and this offers a much less intensive way of modelling the type than this set. Regardless, for its quality alone I can give the PJ conversion set high marks, and it is an interesting and competently produced set that will turn any older FGA.9 kit that you might have to hand into a stock late Swiss Hunter.

Frog F.1 Conversion to P.1067
Kit No. F320

Well, here's a golden oldie! Dating from the mid-50's, this was one of the first kits of the Hunter, and it shows of course. Crude in the extreme, with very little detail, raised panel lines and rivets, a moulded-in pilot's head instead of a cockpit and no gear bays. Why did I bother? Well, to tell the truth, I didn't – this was a fun project all the way. And in these modern times, a lesson in recycling!

Some years ago, I was given an old completed model made from this kit way back when, and put it away as a curiosity. When I started this book project, I pulled it out to have a look and thought I might try bringing it up to reasonable display standards.

First step was to strip off the old paint and decals; with that done, I eliminated all the raised rivets and panel lines, and cut off the crude undercarriage parts. The wings are a very reasonable shape, but require a bit less curve to the outer edges; this took a couple of minutes with a sanding stick. The nose is far too blunt, but about the right length, so this was also attacked with a sanding stick. All cuts and blemishes were repaired with filler.

I was unable to remove the canopy – darn that 1950's glue – so I had to work around it, and live with the pilot's red helmet! It was cleaned up and polished as best I could before being treated with a couple of coats of Future to bring out that certain sparkle.

Frog F.1 converted to P.1067 WB188 – the first Hunter!

At the back end, I ignored the too-sharp taper of the rear fuselage, but I did like the absence of the anti-buffet bullet on the tailplane – and this gave me the idea to finish the model as the P.1067.

Two other features of this aircraft were a shorter canopy – which this kit does in fact feature – and an anti-spin parachute housing above the tailcone. This was created using a small cylindrical bomb found in my spares box which was shortened to the correct length and faired into the tailcone using filler.

I restored a few of the most important panel lines with a scriber then the model was given a coat of primer. With all blemishes removed, I painted the model with RAF Sky, which, according to contemporary sources, is a good approximation of the 'Duck Egg Green' used on the real aircraft. I made the serials, WB188, on my computer and printed them to clear decal paper, then added the oversized roundels that adorned this aircraft, these being scrounged from my spares box.

I had already removed the crude undercarriage and didn't feel like creating new bays, doors and legs from scratch so I decided this would be a flyer. A slot was cut under the fuselage to accept an old Airfix stand. The completed model now sits on one of my bookcases, the perfect 'three-footer!'

While the result is never going to win any competitions, it is a good, and fun, way to re-invent what is an otherwise unremarkable and outdated kit. And I kept it out of the landfill!

Revell 1/144 Hunter FGA.9
Kit No. 04039

This petite kit comes in a side-opening box with nice artwork. Inside, two sprues of grey parts are accompanied by a small clear sprue and a tiny decal sheet offering two options. These are:
- RAF FGA.9 XF523/N of 54 Squadron, RAF West Raynham, 1968,
- Swiss Air Force F.58 J-4102 of Fliegerstaffel 21, 1960.

The instruction booklet has 8 pages. Construction is detailed with exploded diagrams and colour callouts for the details; pretty standard fare. Painting and decalling instructions devote

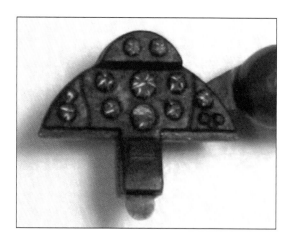

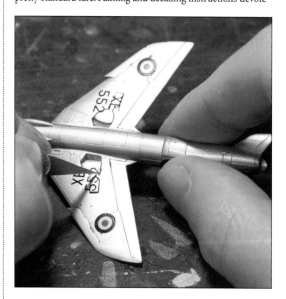

one page each to the two options. Paint recommendations are the standard Revell funky mixes; I prefer Xtracrylix personally.

The parts come on two olive green sprues plus a small clear sprue containing the canopy and a tail prop, but no gunsight. All the parts are cleanly moulded with no flash or obvious defects and the engraved detail is very finely done. The Swiss option does not include any of the later modifications or weapons that can be found in Revell's 1/72 Hunter kit, which is a shame, so

only an early Swiss aircraft can be built from the box.

Construction starts in the cockpit, which features a nice tub with raised side-panel detail. Into this is placed an ejection seat that bears little more than a passing resemblance to the correct Martin-Baker 2H of the RAF's FGA.9 or 3H of the Swiss F.58.

The tub was painted scale black with a light drybrushing of white enamel to highlight the side-panel detail. With the seat fitted and the fuselage halves closed, there's not much to be seen, so I didn't bother creating miniature throttle quadrants and the like. The instrument panel has raised bezel detail and was painted white; once that had dried it was overcoated with scale black. I used a pin to scratch some instrument faces onto the panel. Of course, it was later pointed out to me that the kit's decal sheet has a tiny instrument panel decal…

The tub was glued to the starboard fuselage side, and the fuselage halves joined. Once dried, the lower nose piece, incorporating the nosewheel bay and cannon port detail, was added. The wheel bay is a little shallow, but not enough for me to warrant scratchbuilding a new one! Some small fishing weights were flattened and cut up to fit around the sides of the bay to add some nose weight, and also to the nose cone which is a separate part. Throughout, construction of the fuselage presented no difficulties with just a light sanding required at the seams. The ventral air brake is moulded integrally with the fuselage, which is fine as this unit was normally closed when the aircraft was on the ground.

The wings are simple uppers and lowers with the outboard extended leading edge being moulded integrally, rather than being a separate piece as on their 1/72 kit. However, there is no intake trunking and the area looks quite unrealistic. This was a simple fix. Once the wings had been glued together and had set, some Squadron white putty was added to each intake and smoothed using some nail varnish remover on a cotton bud. After the putty had dried, it was lightly sanded with a small piece of fine sandpaper curled around the end of a paintbrush. This created a nice curved trunk inside each wing. The completed trunks were painted an off-white.

Each completed wing fits into a recess in the fuselage, but before gluing them into place, I painted the recess off-white to match the wing trunking. I added a small circle of black paint about halfway back in each recess; this represents the entry to the engine compressor, and is a perfectly adequate representation in this scale. Once the wings were glued into place, the effect is much more realistic than what the kit provides.

The canopy fits perfectly and was masked with Tamiya tape before I glued it into place.

With main airframe construction complete, it was time to paint this tiny model. After washing with warm water and detergent, the model was allowed to dry thoroughly before a coat of Xtracrylix Dark Sea Grey was added. To compensate for 'scale colour' I added about 25% Medium Sea Grey to lighten it.

To my eye, this looks about right. Once dry, the masking was added and a coat of lightened Dark Green completed the upper camouflage effect.

After allowing the paint to dry overnight, I masked the top surfaces and added a coat of ModelMaster Metalizer Dull Aluminum to the undersides – a relatively flat sheen for scale effect again. This is an important consideration in this scale, as a shiny model would look very toy-like. Having said that, I then proceeded to add a coat of Future acrylic floor wax to give a gloss coat for the decals to sit on!

It had been my original intention to use the kit's decals; however, I quickly found that these were not going to work. I applied the RAF roundels, but was disappointed to find that they wouldn't adhere properly to the model, despite my usually successful method of applying decals over spot-applied wet Future. And the red is a bit bright as well. This was quite unexpected - it might have been a bad batch, as I've had friends build this kit and none had issue with their's – so I acquired a sheet of Xtradecals' 1/144 Worldwide Hunters sheet.

This is an excellent example of the decalmakers' art, offering numerous options, and being well printed. I chose to use the very first option on the sheet, an FGA.9 of the combined 8/43 Squadron, based at RAF Khormaksar during the Aden Conflict in 1966. This features colourful bars on each side of the fuselage roundel, representing 8 Squadron on one side and 43 on the other. These decals work beautifully, being thin and settling down nicely over Future.

With all the decals in place and dried, it was time to add all the fiddly bits, which in this scale are even fiddlier. I was very pleased with the detail on the undercarriage. Both nose and main legs have good detail, and the wheels are little gems. The doors are a bit thick and in retrospect, I should have thinned them. The stores pylons are super, but I noticed a discrepancy with the outer wing pylons. These should line up with the pylon ejector bulges above the wings, but Revell would have you glue them about 2mm inboard of them. It is the pylons that are correctly positioned, so the bulges should be moved to align with the pylons.

The stores selection is a little sparse, but then the FGA.9 wasn't noted for those publicity shots with vast arrays of weapons. The standard 230-gallon drop tanks are included, but these look a bit slim to me and I decided not to use them. Then I managed to lose one of the rocket pods, the carpet monster cleaning up and leaving my little Hunter store-less. The final step was to spray the model with a coat of Xtracrylix Satin Varnish, to give a suitably scaled-down finish.

I am quite pleased with this little model; the kit is very nice indeed – dimensionally very accurate, it features great fit and good detail, and is let down only by the decal sheet.

Revell 1/144 FGA.9 in 8/43 Squadron markings

The main undercarriage in place

The nose gear is nicely detailed for this scale

Hunter Kits

Until quite recently, the Hunter was ill-served by kit manufacturers; while there were a number of kits available, none were of particularly good accuracy. However, the advent of Revell's kits in 1/32, 1/72 and 1/144 has redressed the balance. Here's a listing of Hunter kits that have been available over the years, by scale, followed by listings of Hunter accessories and decals. This list is as comprehensive as possible and my apologies if I have missed any. Companies and products come and go, so these lists should not be taken as an indication that these products are available at the time of reading; it is a guide to what has been available.

1/32

Revell F.6
Kit No. RG 4727 (2006)

Markings Options:
- 1. Hunter F.6, XG239, 92 Sqn, RAF, Middleton St. George, 1958
- 2. Hunter F.6, XF387, 56 Sqn, RAF, Waterbeach, 1960
- 3. Hunter F.6, N-286, 324 Sqn, Royal Netherlands AF, Leeuwarden, 1959-1964
- 4. Hunter F.6, IF126, 22 Sqn, Belgian AF, Bierset, 1960

Revell FGA.9
Kit No. RM 4670/ RG 4703 (1998)

Markings Options (RoG – RM has first 2 only):
- 1. Hunter FGA.9, XF376, 208 Sqn, RAF, Kuwait, 1961
- 2. Hunter FGA.9, XK137, 45 Sqn, RAF, Wittering, 1976
- 3. Hunter F.58, Patrouille Suisse, Swiss AF, Dubendorf AB, 1991
- 4. Hunter F.58, J-4068, Fliegerstaffel 20, Swiss AF, Mollis AB, 1993

First released in 1998, the large scale Hunter FGA.9 is a very nice, relatively unsophisticated kit. Molded in light gray plastic, the kit features 172 parts on six parts trees, plus a single sprue of clear parts. The kit features a nicely detailed cockpit, positionable flaps, landing gear and speed brake, positionable canopy, large external tanks on the inboard pylons, flattened tires, and a choice of smaller external tanks or rocket pods on the outboard pylons. It is cleanly moulded and accuracy is excellent – the only issue is that the dogtooth is 2mm too far outboard. The majority of the parts are common to the F.6 kit as well – it is

the tailcone and landing flaps that are different between the two types.

The Revell-Monogram Hawker Hunter FGA.9 is a repackaged version of the Hunter FGA.9/F.58 kit released in Europe by Revell of Germany. Unfortunately, the US release does not include the parts or decals to model the Swiss Hunter F.58, which included a pair of AGM-65 Maverick missiles. This is disappointing, but overall, these are very nice kits and the resulting model is very impressive.

Echelon Single-seater/Two-seater Kits

Markings Options (Single-seater)
- 1. F.4 WW663/H, 14 Sqn
- 2. F.6 XE616/F, 1 Sqn
- 3. FGA.9 XE651/L, 1 Sqn
- 4. F.5 WP130/S, 34 Sqn
- 5. FR.10 XE580/D, 4 Sqn
- 6. GA.11 WT804, FAA Blue Herons

Echelon produced two large-scale vacform kits in the mid-1980s; one enabled the modeller to produce many of the single-seater marks with alternate tailcones and wing leading edge extensions, the other to create either the T.7 and 8. These were moulded on 4 sheets with around 80 parts and included white metal parts for many of the smaller details. Full decal sheets were included.

Apparently accurate and relatively easy to build, these are now quite rare and I was unable to acquire one of these limited-run kits.

1/48

Academy F.6
Kit No. 2164

Markings Option:
• 1. F.6 XE597, 63 Sqn RAF

Academy FGA.9
Kit No. 2169

Markings Options:
• 1. FGA.9 XE655, 8 Sqn RAF, 1961
• 2. FGA.57 213, Kuwaiti AF, 1966

These two are real 'curate's eggs'. Heralded as the first modern 1/48 Hunter kits when they were released in 1997, these are excellent kits that actually build up quite well; however, their accuracy leaves a lot to be desired! Please see the preceding chapter for more details on the many issues with this kit, and how to correct them.

Nichimo 1/48

Aeroclub F.4/5
Kit No. K420

Marking Options
• 1. 112 Sqn RAF
• 2. 1(F) Sqn RAF

Aeroclub F.6
Kit No. K421

Markings Options
• 1. 247 Sqn RAF
• 2. 19 Sqn RAF

Aeroclub T.7/8
Kit No. K422

Markings Options
• 1. 237 OCU RAF
• 2. Flag Officer Training, FAA

Aeroclub FGA.9
Kit No. K423

Markings Options
• 1. 79 Sqn RAF
• 2. 8 Sqn RAF

Aeroclub produced these four mixed-media kits featuring vacform fuselage and wings, combined with injection moulded leading edges, wingtips, ailerons, flaps, air intakes and the tail group, along with white metal undercarriage and cockpit parts. A clear vacform canopy was included, and decals included a separate common sheet for national markings and serials. Widely lauded as the most accurate Hunters available in 1/48, unfortunately they have been unavailable for some years and are now very desirable.

ID Models F.6

No decals included. This vacform model dates from 1981 and consisted of one large sheet of parts plus a smaller sheet for wheels, seat, cockpit detail and undercarriage – all in vacformed plastic – no white metal parts were included. I haven't seen one in person, but looking at photos of completed models, accuracy appears to be quite good, although the canopy appears to be set too deep into the nose.

Hard to come by nowadays, but occasionally pops up on internet auction sites.

Lindberg F.6(?)
Marking Option:
• 1. WT585, 43 Squadron – this was actually an F.1, but did serve with 43!

One of the first Hunter kits to be released, this one has surfaced many times over the years, and with the recent revival of Lindberg, we may well see it again. This one is a creature of its times, and has a host of working features, including a detachable rear fuselage to show off a rather generic jet engine. It is also the only kit to feature the experimental thrust reversers fitted to XF833. A pair of drop tanks is included, as are a pair of bizarre AAMs! The big surprise with this kit is that dimensionally, it's not all that bad! The front fuselage, up to the point where the kit breaks at the transport joint, is actually very good in outline, while the wings, to Mod.228 with 4 pylons, dog-tooth and extended leading edge, are acceptable with some work. Of course, you'll need to eliminate the 1950's surface detail, rivets and all, and add detail to taste, but it's a reasonable starting point. However, the rear fuselage is a big problem, as it is too pinched. I suppose you could correct it starting with the Aeroclub tailcone parts – and use the rest of that correction set on the rest of the kit, which needs a lot of help with the cockpit and undercarriage. If you find this kit going cheap, don't dismiss it out of hand! This kit was also released by Nichimo and UPC under their own labels.

Merit F.1

Perhaps the first Hunter kit ever released, way back in the mid-fifties, this one is a real collector's item, and is another I have unfortunately never seen.

Airfix F.6
Kit No. 2006

Markings Option:
• 1. F.6, XF416/T, 111 Sqn RAF 'Black Arrows'

Originally released back in 1960, the kit originally featured a separate cannon pack as its token 'working feature!' Not particularly accurate, the fuselage is wrongly proportioned and the wings are incorrectly placed in relation to it. The issue here is that the length between the cockpit and intakes is about 4mm too great, throwing everything off – not much can reasonably be done to correct this, and there are better kits available today. The nose is too pointed and too short ahead of the cockpit. The wings are OK in shape, but the dogtooth is too far out on the wing and incorrectly angled. The tailcone is too pinched. Detail is poor by modern standards, particularly the undercarriage, and the decals are very basic.

Airfix FGA.9
Kit No. 2073

Markings Options:
1980's
• 1. FGA.9, XJ673/XX, 20 Sqn RAF, 1962
• 2. FGA.57, 212, Kuwaiti AF
1990's
• 1. FGA.9, XJ673/XX, 20 Sqn RAF, 1962
• 2. F.9, XE624, 79 Sqn RAF, 1972

This was a revised version of the old F.6 kit, but dimensionally has not been improved – see the comments above under F.6.

Frog F.1
Kit No. F320

Markings Options:
• 1. F.1, 43 Squadron

One of the earliest Hunter kits and very crude by today's standards. There is no detail to speak of, the 'cockpit' is moulded over and there is a half-pilot sticking up from the blank. There are no undercarriage bays and the gear is moulded all in one piece to fit into slots under the wings and nose. Surface detail is raised lines and rivets. The intakes are very poor, with a see-through effect both along and across the fuselage! Decals are very basic and offer just one option.

Despite this, the model is not terribly inaccurate in shape and dimension. The nose is too blunt and the wings need some reshaping, while the tailcone needs some work. Of course, it has been superseded by most of the later kits, but with some effort, a nice desktop model can be produced! Note: Also issued by Novo with the same kit no. and markings, and by Eastern Express with 54 Squadron markings.

Frog FGA.9
Kit No. F204

Markings Options:
• 1. FGA.9, XJ642, 54 Sqn RAF, 1968
• 2. F.58, J-4078, FlSt.1 Swiss AF, 1964

A brand new mould rather than a revision of the very old F.1, and it shows in its better detail, but not necessarily in accuracy. The wings are very poor, being far too broad outboard of the dogtooth. The nose is too short and skinny, while the cockpit sits too low in the fuselage. The fuselage itself is a little chubby, while the intakes are a bit small.

There is an open cockpit, but not much to go inside, while the undercarriage is very basic. Overall, it is a fair kit, but needs quite a bit of work to bring it up to a reasonable display model.

Eastern Express F.1
Kit No. 72272

Markings Option:
• 1. F.1, WW636/Q, 54 Sqn RAF, 1955

This is the old Frog F.1 kit – see above for remarks.

Matchbox T.7/F.6
Kit No. PK117

Markings Options:
1976 Release
• 1. T.7, XL619, 45 Sqn RAF, 1974
• 2. F.6A, XE651, 58 Sqn RAF, 1974
1983 Release
• 1. T.7, 92 Sqn RAF 'Blue Diamonds'
• 2. F.6A, XE651, 58 Sqn RAF, 1974
Note: Some later boxings included markings for a Swiss AF F.58.

The only mainstream kit to include a two-seater option, that's really all that this kit has going for it, and even then, it's work. Released in 1975, the Matchbox Hunter has separate nose sections for the F.6 and T.7, but each is rather inaccurate, being too wide and too long. Both canopies are too large and poorly shaped. The tail end features a rather small and indistinct brake parachute housing and an odd looking tailcone. The wings are much too broad outboard of the dogtooth, and the intakes are see-through. Detail is virtually non-existent, and surface detail is very heavy trench-like engraved lines. This one needs major work to bring it up to scratch.

PJ Production F.4 Belgian Air Force
Kit No. 721014

PJ Production F.6/FR.10/FR.57
Kit No. 721022

PJ Production's Hunter kits are complete resin kits with decals, and will build into very nice models – in fact, I consider them to be ideal first resin kits, such is the ease of construction. While the models look very good, they are about 2mm off on span and length, and I think there may have been issues with resin shrinkage with the sample I had – hopefully, these were isolated cases.

Plastyk F.6
Kit No. S-007

Markings Options:
- 1. F.6A XE606, 1TWU RAF
- 2. FGA.71 J704, 9 Grupo, Chilean AF
- 3. FGA.71, J737, 8 Grupo, Chilean AF, 1971

Often written off as a Frog clone, with some features that resemble the FGA.9 kit, this was in fact a new tool. Detail is very basic, but the panel lines are engraved rather than raised. Dimensionally, the kit is about 2mm too short, but the wings are very good in shape and span. The big issue is the rear fuselage that features a very constipated tailcone! The issue is that the rear fuselage tapers in much too much and too soon, giving a rather odd pinched look to the back end. Other than surgery, there's not much to be done here. The decals look pretty poor, but as I didn't make the kit, I don't know for sure. Overall, rather disappointing, but I suppose one could try cross-kitting the Airfix rear fuselage onto the rest of this kit, making the cut at the rear transport joint.

Revell F.6
Kit No. 04350

Markings Options:
- 1. F.6 XG204, Fighter Combat School, RAF, 1961
- 2. F.6 XF462, 66Sqn RAD, 1959
- 3. F.6 N-283, 324 Sqn RNethAF, 1957
- 4. F.6 IF-126/IS-U, 22 Sqn Belgian AF, 1960

Revell FGA.9
Kit No. 04186

Markings Options:
- 1. FGA.9, 1TWU RAF, 1979
- 2. FGA.9, 79 Sqn RAF, 1984
- 3. F.58, 'Patrouille Suisse' Swiss AF, 1991
- 4. F.58, FlSt.20 Swiss AF, 1993

Revell's new F.6 and FGA.9 kits are excellent examples of the modern kit maker's art, being simple, accurate and very reasonably priced. There is a good variety of markings options in each kit and there really isn't much need for aftermarket items to complete these kits to a very nice standard. Details such as the cockpit and undercarriage are very nicely rendered, while there is a reasonable selection of stores. My only concerns are that the dogtooth is a touch too far outboard on the wing, and the intake areas are simple openings without any attempt to show the curved trunking.

If you are in the market for a 1/72 Hunter, these two kits are the ones to get. Now, if Revell would think about an early Hunter…

1/144

Revell FGA.9
Kit No. 04039

Marking Options:
- 1. FGA.9, XF523, 54 Sqn. RAF, 1968
- 2. F.58, J-4102, FlSt.21 Swiss AF

This is a decent little kit, a modern 1/144 scale kit with actual cockpit detail! Fit is very good and detail excellent for the scale, although the intakes are just an open space. Very good in regards to accuracy, but lacks variety in weaponry especially for the Swiss version.

Welsh Models F.6
Kit No. PJW2-1

I was unable to obtain one of these vacform kits, but I am told that it was quite accurate. In addition to the IM parts, the kit contained a white metal undercarriage, vacform canopy and a small decal sheet.

Airfix/Craftmaster 1/72 F.6

Hunter Accessories

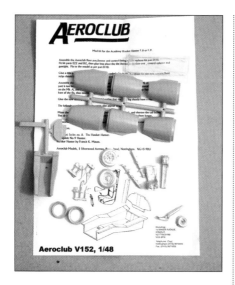

Aeroclub 1/48 correction set

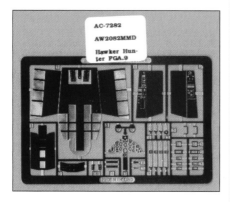

Airwaves 1/72 PE set

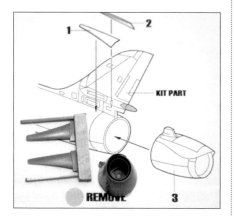

Quickboost 1/72 FGA.9 conversion set for Revell

COMPANY	STOCK #	SCALE	MATERIAL	DESCRIPTION
A2Zee	n/a	1/72	resin	PR.10/GA.11 conversion set
Aeroclub	C023	1/72	vac	Hunter single-seater Canopy
	C024	1/72	vac	Hunter two-seater Canopy
	C073	1/48	vac	Hunter single-seater canopy
	EJ008	1/72	wm	Martin-Baker Mk.3 seat
	EJ010	1/72	wm	Martin-Baker Mk.4 seat for T.7/8
	EJ402	1/48	wm	Martin-Baker Mk.3 seat
	EJ403	1/48	wm	Martin-Baker Mk.4 seat for T.7/8
	EJ302	1/32	resin	Martin-Baker Mk.2H seat
	EJ303	1/32	resin	Martin-Baker Mk.3H seat
	EJ423	1/48	resin	Martin-Baker Mk.2H seat
	V152	1/48	mixed	Hunter correction set
	V157	1/48	wm	Hunter undercarriage set
	V186	1/32	wm	Hunter undercarriage legs
	V233	1/72	wm	Hunter undercarriage set
	VA58	1/72	vac	T.7 correction for Matchbox
	VA59	1/72	vac	F.6 correction for Matchbox
Airwaves	72082	1/72	pe	Hunter FGA.9 photo etch set
	72087	1/72	pe	Hunter FGA.9 PE flaps & airbrake
	32001	1/32	resin	Martin-Baker Mk.3 seat
	48025	1/48	wm	Martin-Baker Mk.4 seat for T.7/8
	48082	1/48	pe	Hunter PE set
	48119	1/48	resin	Hunter Mk 1/2 conversion set
Aires	4085	1/48	resin	Hunter cockpit
	4087	1/48	resin	Hunter wheel bays
	4130	1/48	resin	Hunter FGA.9 detail set
CAM Resin	32035	1/32	resin	Martin-Baker Mk.2H seat
	32036	1/32	resin	Martin-Baker Mk.3H seat
Cutting Edge	48115	1/48	resin	Hunter F.6/FGA.9 cockpit
CzechMaster	7123	1/72	resin	Hunter interior set
	7124	1/72	resin	Hunter exterior set
	7125	1/72	resin	Hunter undercarriage set
Eduard	32037	1/32	pe	Hunter detail set
	48233	1/48	pe	Hunter F.6 detail set
	73230	1/72	pe	Hunter F.6 detail set pre-painted
	X105	1/72		Hunter single-seater paint mask
	X045	1/48		Hunter single-seater paint mask
	X025	1/32		Hunter single-seater paint mask
	SS230	1/72	pe	Hunter F.6 detail set zoom
Fisher Models		1/32	resin	Hunter T.7 conversion set
Flightpath	32003	1/32	resin	Hunter detail set
	32004	1/32	resin	Hunter diorama set
	32005	1/32	resin	Hunter F.4/5/GA.11 conversion
	48046	1/48	mixed	Hunter super-detail set
	48056	1/48	mixed	Hunter detail/weapons set
	72046	1/72	mixed	Hunter detail set
	72063	1/72	pe	Hunter ladder
	72067	1/72	pe	Hunter detail set

COMPANY	STOCK #	SCALE	MATERIAL	DESCRIPTION
Falcon	4048	1/48	vac	RAF canopies, inc. Hunter
Neomega	C16	1/48	resin	Hunter cockpit set
	E14/48	1/48	resin	Martin-Baker Mk.2 seat
Pavla	C7249	1/72	mixed	Hunter F.6 detail set
	S7239	1/72	resin	Martin-Baker Mk.3H
	U7268	1/72	resin	Hunter prototype conversion
	U7289	1/72	resin	Hunter F.3 conversion
PJ Production	481202	1/48	resin	Martin-Baker 2H
	481203	1/48	resin	Martin-Baker 3H
	481207	1/48	resin	Hunter F.58 conversion
	481208	1/48	resin	Hunter FR.10 conversion
	481209	1/48	resin	Hunter GA.11 conversion
	721202	1/72	resin	Hunter F.58 conversion
	721204	1/72	resin	Martin-Baker 2H
	721205	1/72	resin	Martin-Baker 3H
	721207	1/72	resin	Hunter T.7/8/68 conversion
PP Aeroparts	717	1/72	pe	Hunter Ladder
Quickboost	72111	1/72	resin	Hunter FGA.9 conversion
	72115	1/72	resin	Hunter air brake
	72129	1/72	resin	Hunter reconnaissance nose
True Details	32453	1/32	resin	Hunter cockpit detail set
	48423	1/48	resin	Martin-Baker 2H
	49007	1/48	resin	Hunter F.6 cockpit
Wolfpack	WP72022	1/72	resin	F.3 conversion set
	WP48029	1/48	resin	F.1/2/4/5 conversion set
	WP48057	1/48	resin	F.3 conversion set
Whirlybirds	WBA4401	1/144	resin	T.7 conversion

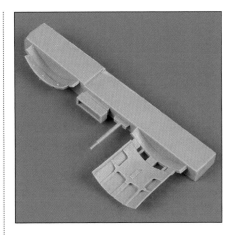

Quickboost 1/72 air brake set

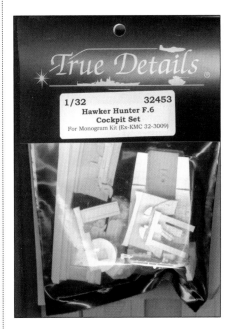

True Details 1/32 cockpit set

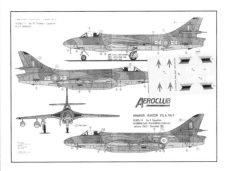

Aeroclub D012 1/48

Hunter Decals

COMPANY	STOCK #	SCALE	DESCRIPTION
Almark	S01	1/72	inc. decals for Rough Diamonds GA.11
Aeroclub	D010	1/48	F.4/5
	D011	1/48	F.6
	D012	1/48	FGA.9
Aeromaster	32001	1/32	RAF & Chile
	32002	1/32	RAF FR.10
	32003	1/32	RAF, Abu Dhabi, Oman, Zimbabwe
	32004	1/32	India, Switzerland, Singapore
	48345	1/48	RAF F.4/5/6
	48346	1/48	
	48347	1/48	
Aztec	7207	1/72	inc. Chile FGA.71
Carpena	48099	1/48	
	72037	1/72	
Cutting Edge	72043	1/72	
	72044	1/72	
	48043	1/48	
	48044	1/48	RAF, RN, ETPS, Switzerland, India

Aeromaster 32001

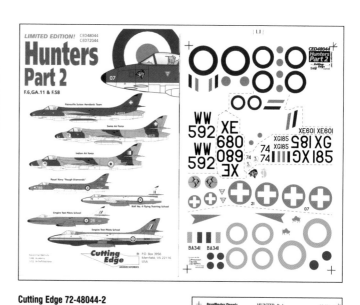

Cutting Edge 72-48044-2

Aeromaster 32002

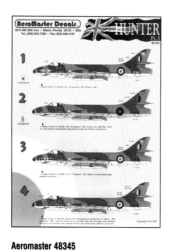

Aeromaster 32004

Aeromaster 32003

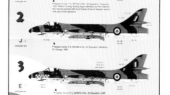

Aeromaster 48345

Aeromaster 48346

Aeromaster 32001-2

COMPANY	STOCK #	SCALE	DESCRIPTION
Daco	DCD3243	1/32	Diables Rouge, Belgian Roundels & Stencils
	DCD3244	1/32	Belgian Hunter Squadron Codes & Numbers
	DCD4843	1/48	Belgian Hunter Roundels & Stencils
	DCD4844	1/48	Belgian Hunter Squadron Codes & Numbers
	DCD4845	1/48	Diables Rouge
	DCD7243	1/72	Belgian Hunter Roundels & Stencils
	DCD7244	1/72	Belgian Hunter Squadron Codes & Numbers
	DCD7245	1/72	Diables Rouge
Dutch Decals	72007	1/72	Dutch T.7
	72020	1/72	Dutch F.4/6; 322, 323, 324, 325 Sqns
Esci	86	1/72	inc. RAF, India, Iraq, Jordan
Flightpath	48056A	1/48	RAF FGA.9s
Maestro Decals	72-003	1/72	inc. Swedish F.50
ModelArt	48-003	1/48	
	72-008	1/72	inc. RN GA.11, T.7/8C/8M
	72-009	1/72	inc. RN T.8, Swiss F.58 x 2
	72-010	1/72	inc. RN GA.11, Danish F.51
	72-050	1/72	inc. RN T.8
	72-055	1/72	inc. Swiss and Jordanian Hunters
	72-056	1/72	inc. RN Hunter GA.11s
	144-001	1/144	RAF, RN & International Hunters

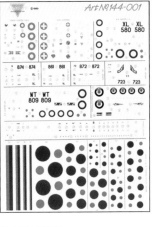

Model Art 144001

Cutting Edge 72-48044

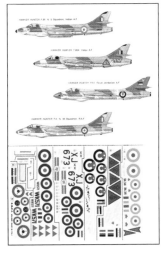

Esci 86

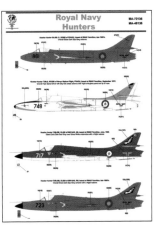

Model Alliance 48136

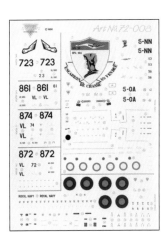

Model Art 72008

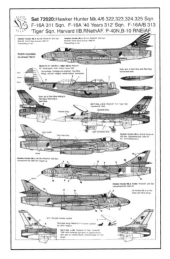

Dutch Decal 72020

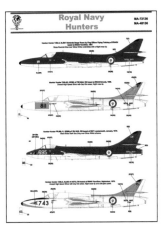

Model Alliance 48136

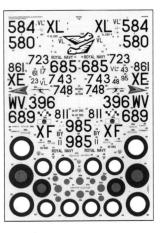

Model Alliance 48136

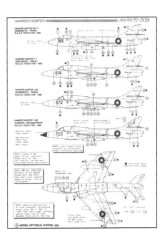

Model Art 72008

Model Art 72056-01

COMPANY	STOCK #	SCALE	DESCRIPTION
Modeldecal	7	1/72	inc. RAF F.6
	25	1/72	inc. RAF FGA.9
	26	1/72	inc. RAF FGA.9
	28	1/72	inc. RN T.8
	86	1/72	RAF F.4/5/6/FGA.9/FR.10
Model Alliance	48136	1/48	Royal Navy Hunters
	72136	1/72	Senior Service Hunters
RAFDec	7213	1/72	RAF Hunters F.2/4/5/6, FGA.9
Superscale	720548	1/72	RAF Hunters FGA.9/FR.10/T.7
	720549	1/72	RAF Hunters FGA.9/FR.10/T.7
Xtradecal	32007	1/32	Hunter F.6
	00532	1/32	Hunter FGA.9
	44003	1/144	Hunters RAF & Foreign
	48033	1/48	Hunter F.6
	48034	1/48	Hunter FGA.9/FR.10
	72046	1/72	Hunter F.6
	72047	1/72	Hunter FGA.9/FR.10
	72058	1/72	Hunter F.6 inc,. Dutch, Belgian, Jordan
	72063	1/72	International Hunters

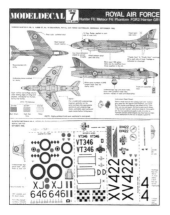

Modeldecal 7

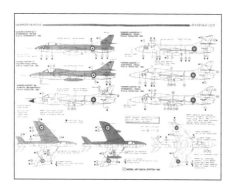

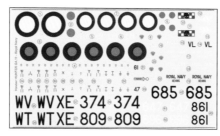

Model Art 72056-02

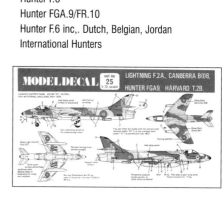

Modeldecal 25

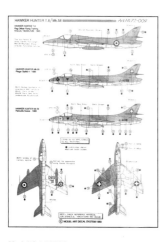

Model Art 144001-02

Modeldecal 26

Modeldecal 28

Model Art 72009

Modeldecal 86

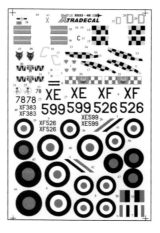

Xtradecal 03348

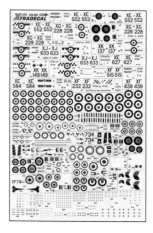

Xtradecal 44003

Hunter Specifications

GENERAL SPECIFICATIONS (F.6 – see table below for other marks)

Length:	45 ft 11 in (14.00 m)
Wingspan:	33 ft 8 in (10.26 m)
Height:	13 ft 2 in (4.01 m)
Wing area:	349 ft² (32.42 m²)
Empty weight:	14,122 lb (6,405 kg)
Loaded weight:	17,750 lb (8050 kg)
Max takeoff weight:	24,600 lb (11,158 kg)
Fuel Capacity:	390 gallons internal, 400 gallons external.
Powerplant:	1× Rolls-Royce Avon 203, 10,145 lb thrust (45.13 kN)

PERFORMANCE

Maximum speed:	Mach 0.94, 620 knots (715 mph, 1,150 km/h) at sea level
Combat range:	385 nm (445 mi, 715 km)
Ferry range:	1,650 nm (1,900 mi, 3,060 km) with external fuel
Service ceiling:	50,000 ft (15,240 m)
Rate of climb:	17,200 ft/min (87.4 m/s)
Wing loading:	51.6 lb/ft² (251.9 kg/m²)

ARMAMENT

4x 30 mm ADEN cannon, 120 rounds per gun; guns fitted into a removable gun pack under the front fuselage
Up to 7,400 lb (3400 kg) of weapons on four hardpoints including SNEB 68 mm rockets in 18-round Matra pods, SURA rockets, up to 1,000lb bombs, or 100-gallon drop tanks.
Some export Hunters, notably those of Singapore, Oman and Switzerland, were modified to carry AIM-9 Sidewinder or AGM-65 Maverick.

AVIONICS

Ekco Ranging radar
TR1986 and TR1987 VHF radios (ARC52 UHF radios on later aircraft)

The Hunter airframe varied relatively little over the course of its development. Of course, larger engines were fitted, and the extended leading edge was fitted to later marks, but the airframe changed remarkably little otherwise. Export aircraft were slightly modified from the marks listed below, as noted in Chapter 3.

XE601, the last UK military Hunter, also seen at Boscombe Down, where she served with the A&AEE for many years
(© via Andy Evans)

	FIRST FLIGHT	ENGINE	EMPTY WEIGHT	MAX. WEIGHT	LENGTH	SPAN	WING AREA	HEIGHT
P.1067	20-Jul-51	Avon 103, 6,500 lb			45' 11"	33' 8"	340 sq ft	13' 2"
F.1	16-May-53	Avon 113, 7,500 lb	12,128 lb	16,200 lb	45' 11"	33' 8"	340 sq ft	13' 2"
F.2	14-Oct-53	Sapphire 101, 8,000 lb	12128 lb	16,200 lb	45' 11"	33' 8"	340 sq ft	13' 2"
F.3	12-Aug-53	RA.7R Avon, 9,600 lb				33' 8"	340 sq ft	13' 2"
F.4	19-Oct-54	Avon 113-121, 7,500-8,000 lb	12,543 lb	17,100 lb	45' 11"	33' 8"	340 sq ft	13' 2"
F.5	20-Oct-54	Sapphire 101, 8,000 lb	12,543 lb	17,100 lb	45' 11"	33' 8"	340 sq ft	13' 2"
F.6	23-May-55	Avon 203-207, 10,000 lb	12,760 lb	17,750 lb	45' 11"	33' 8"	349 sq ft	13' 2"
T.7	8-Jul-55	Avon 122, 7,450 lb	13,360 lb	17,200 lb	48' 10"	33' 8"	349 sq ft	13' 2"
T.8	3-Mar-58	Avon 122, 7,450 lb	13,480 lb	17,200 lb	48' 10"	33' 8"	349 sq ft	13' 2"
FGA.9	3 July 1859	Avon 207, 10,050 lb	13,010 lb	18,000 lb	45' 11"	33' 8"	349 sq ft	13' 2"
FR.10	7-Nov-59	Avon 207, 10,050 lb	13,100 lb	18,100 lb	46' 1"	33' 8"	349 sq ft	13' 2"
GA.11		Avon 121, 8,000 lb	12,600 lb	17,100 lb	45' 11"	33' 8"	349 sq ft	13' 2"

RAF Users of the Hunter

UNIT	MARK	DATE USED	BASE	EXAMPLE A/C	NOTES
1	F.5	9/55-23/6/58	Tangmere	WN973/B, WP119/T	
	F.6	1/7/58-3/60	Stradishall	XE616/E	
	FGA.9	1/60-8/63	Waterbeach	XE624/B	
		8/63-7/69	West Raynham		
2	FR.10	3/61-3/71	Gutersloh	XE556/W, XE585/E	
3	F.4	5/56-6/57	Geilenkirchen	XF949/C, XF990/K	
4	F.4	7/55-9/57	Jever	WV266/T, WV275/D	
	F.6	2/57-30/12/60	Jever	XE548/H	
	FR.10	1/1/61-30/5/70	Gutersloh	XE580/D, XE650/E	renumbered from 79 Sqn
8	FGA.9	1/60-12/71	Khormaksar	XE651/M, XG128/Q	
12	T.7	10/69-10-93	Honington		Used as training and standards a/c on a Buccaneer sqn.
			Lossiemouth		
14	F.4	5/55-4/57	Oldenburg	WW663/H	
	F.6	4/57-12/62	Ahlhorn	XJ691/M, XJ712/B	
			Gutersloh		
			Jever		
15	T.7	10/70-9/83	Laarbruch		Used as training and standards a/c on a Buccaneer sqn.
16	T.7	1/73-1/3/84	Laarbruch		
19	F.6	10/56-6/59	Church Fenton	XF449/S, XG172/B	
		6/59-11/62	Leconfield		
20	F.4	11/55-6/57	Oldenburg	WV391/Z	
	F.6	5/57/57-30/8/58	Ahlhorn	XG128/Y, XJ680/A	
		30/8/58-30/12/60	Gutersloh		
	FGA.9	1/9/61-18/2/70	Tengah	XJ673/XX	
26	F.4	6/55-15/9/57	Oldenburg	WV410/B	
	F.6	1/58-30/12/60	Gutersloh	XF415/J	
28	FGA.9	7/62-2/1/67	Kai Tak	XE622/A, XG297/B	
34	F.5	10/55-10/1/58	Tangmere	WP130/S, WP185/E	
41	F.5	7/55-31/1/58	Biggin Hill	WN966/M, WP122/A	
43	F.1	7/54-8/56	Leuchars	WT622/G, WW645/S	1st Operational Hunter Squadron
	F.4	3/56-7/58	Leuchars	WV387/Q, XE663/V	
	F.6	12/56-7/60	Leuchars	XE560/G, XF456/A	
	FGA.9	4/60-3/63	Leuchars	XE552/D, XE611/X	
		6/61-3/63	Nicosia		
		3/63-7/11/67	Khormaksar		
45	FGA.9	1/8/72-26/7/76	Wittering	XG130/61, XK137/66	
54	F.1	2/55-10/55	Odiham	WW636/Q, WT692/S	
	F.4	9/55-1/57	Odiham	WV281/M	
	F.6	1/57-3/60	Stradishall	XG273/L	
	FGA.9	3/60-9/69	West Raynham	XF523/N	
56	F.5	5/55-11/58	Waterbeach	WP104/A, WP123/B	
	F.6	11/58-7/59	Waterbeach	XF387/D	
		7/59-1/61	Wattisham		
58	FGA.9	1/8/73-4/6/76	Wittering	XE651/87, XF442/81	
63	F.6	11/56-10/58	Waterbeach	XE597/A, XE647/E	
	F.6/FGA.9	1/6/63-1/9/74	Chivenor		229 OCU shadow Sqn - see entry below
		2/9/74-5/79	Brawdy		TWU/1TWU shadow Sqn
65	F.6	12/56-3/61	Duxford	XF447/H, XF507/A	
66	F.4	3/56-10/56	Linton-on-Ouse	WT809/G, XF304/B	
	F.6	10/56-30/9/60	Acklington	XG253/A, XK139/G	
67	F.4	1/56-4/57	Bruggen	XF296/Z, XF317/U	
71	F.4	5/56-30/4/57	Bruggen	XF313/G	
74	F.4	3/57-1/58	Horsham St. Faith	WV334/E, XG683/G	
	F.6	11/57-6/59	Horsham St. Faith	XF511/P, XG198/Q	
		6/59-11/60	Coltishall		
79	F.6, FGA.9, FR.10	1/67-1984	Chivenor		229 OCU/1TWU shadow Sqn
92	F.4	4/56-3/57	Linton-on-Ouse	WV314/B, XF324/D	
	F.6	2/57-4/63	Middleton St. George	XG226/B, XG232/G	Blue Diamonds 1961-2

UNIT	MARK	DATE USED	BASE	EXAMPLE A/C	NOTES
93	F.4	1/56-2/58	Jever	WV267/R, XE718/A	
	F.6	2/58-12/60	Jever	"XE550/R, XJ717/Z"	
98	F.4	3/55-15/7/57	Jever	WW656/N, WW658/O	
111	F.4	6/55-11/56	North Weald	WT716/D, WT811/H	
	F.6	11/56-3/58	North Weald	XF506/X, XJ715/H	Black Arrows 1958-60
		3/58-6/58	North Luffenham		
		6/58-4/61	Wattisham		
112	F.4	5/56-31/5/57	Bruggen	XF319/?, XF937/T	
118	F.4	3/55-31/7/57	Jever	WT743/R, WT748/S	Sqn may have operated a few F.6
127					229 OCU shadow Sqn - see entry below
130	F.4	4/56-5/57	Bruggen	XF294/B, XF295/C	
131					229 OCU shadow Sqn - see entry below
145					229 OCU shadow Sqn - see entry below
208	F.5	1/58-2/58	Tangmere		
	F.6	2/58-31/3/59	Tangmere	XF441/P, XJ694/D	
	FGA.9	3/60-11/61	Nairobi	XG169/K, XJ632/B	
		11/61-6/64	Khormaksar		
		6/64-9/71	Muharraq		
	F.6A/T.7	10/74-31/3/94	Lossiemouth		Used as training and standards a/c on a Buccaneer sqn.
216					Used as training and standards a/c on a Buccaneer sqn.
222	F.1	12/54-8/56	Leuchars	WT615/O	2nd Operational Hunter Squadron
	F.4	8/56-1/11/57	Leuchars	WV372/H, WV399/B	
234	F.4	5/56-15/7/57	Geilenkirchen	WV363/K, XE689/K	
	T.7	1958-80			229OCU/TWU shadow sqn
245	F.4	3/57-6/57	Stradishall	WV330/D, XE687/G	
247	F.1	6/55-7/55	Odiham	WW638/J	
	F.4	7/55-3/57	Odiham	WT768/G, WV317/S	
	F.6	3/57-12/57	Odiham	XE581/T, XF424/V	
257	F.2	11/54-31/3/57	Wattisham	WN907/H, WN950/F	
263	F.2	1/55-10/57	Wattisham	WN921/S, WN981/V	
	F.5	2/55-10/57	Wattisham	WN981/V, WP108/T	
	F.6	10/57-23/6/58	Stradishall		renumbered no.1 Sqn, 23/6/58
229 OCU	F.1, F.4, F.6, FGA.9, FR.10, T.7	2/55-1/9/74	Chivenor		63, 79, 127, 131, 145, 234 - shadow sqns
233 OCU	F.1	1956-57	Pembrey	WW604/F	
237 OCU	T.7, T.8	1/3/71-1/10/91	Honington	XF967/XC	Buccaneer Conversion Unit
TWU	F.6, T.7, FGA.9	2/9/74-30/7/78	Brawdy		
1 TWU	F.6, T.7, FGA.9	30/7/78-9/84	Brawdy		
2 TWU	F.6, T.7, FGA.9	30/7/78-5/81	Lossiemouth		
1417 Flt	FR.10/T.7	1/3/63-8/6/67	Khormaksar	XF460/KS, XF321/TZ	Detached from 8 Sqn
4 FTS	F.6/T.7	1967-76	Valley	XG274/71, XL597/87	
Harrier Conv Flt	FGA.9	1/1/69-1//70	Wittering	XF430/N	
Central Fighter Est.	F.1, F.2, F.4, F.5, F.6, T.7, FGA.9	5/54-10/62	West Raynham		inc. AFDS & DFLS
		10/62-1/2/66	Binbrook		
Fighter Weapons School	F.1	1/1/55-3/3/58	Leconfield	WT614/B	
Central Flying School	F.1, F.4, F.6, T.7	1954-late 1960's			
ETPS	F.1, F.4, F.6, T.7	mid1950's-mid1990's	Boscombe Down	XF375/6, XL564/4	

Notes

1. Sqns may have operated different marks, indeed, different types during transition periods.

2. From 1959, most squadrons operated at least one T.7 two-seat trainer for pilot training.

3. Buccaneer squadrons used T.7s as trainers; also F.6 and FGA.9s in 1980-1 when Buccaneers were grounded.

Sources

Fighter Squadrons of the RAF and Their Aircraft, John Rawlings, Macdonald, 1969

Hunter Squadrons of the Royal Air Force and Fleet Air Arm, Richard L. Ward, Linewrights, 1985

Wings of Fame Volume 20, article by Jon Lake, Aerospace Publishing, 2000"

Scale Aircraft Modelling, Vol.2 No. 4, article by Paul A. Jackson, Alan W. Hall Publications, 1980

RAF Squadrons, Wg Cdr CG Jefford, Airlife, 1988

Hunter Bibliography

Hawker Hunter - Biography of a Thoroughbred,
Francis K Mason
PSL, 1981

Hawker Hunter – The Operational Record
Robert Jackson
Airlife, 1989

Wings of Fame volume 20
Jon Lake
Aerospace Publishing, 2000

Hunter F Mk 6 and T Mk 7 – Aeroguide 9
Roger Chesneau
Linewrights, 1985

Hawker Hunter in Action 121
Glenn Ashley
Squadron/Signal, 1992

Hawker Hunter in Color
Robbie Robinson
Squadron/Signal, 1986

Hunter Squadrons of the Royal Air Force and Fleet Air Arm
Richard Ward
Linewrights, 1985

Hawker Hunter Warpaint No.8
Alan W Hall
Hall Park, 1999

Royal Air Force Germany Since 1945
Bill Taylor
Midland, 2003

Hawker Hunter F.6 Profile No.4
Francis K Mason
Profile Publications, 1964

Hawker Hunter Super Profile
MJ Hardy
Haynes, 1985

Hawker Hunter Two-Seaters Profile No.167
Francis K. Mason
Profile Publications, 1967

Hawker Hunter F.1-T.66 in Royal Air Force & Foreign Service (Aircam No. 26)
Francis K Mason
Osprey, 1971

Famous Airplanes of the World #66 Hawker Hunter
Bunrin-Do, 1997

Hawker Hunter In Dienst Bij De Belgische Luchtmacht/Au Service de L'Aviation Belge,
Andre van Haute
Uitgeverij De Krijger, 1996/2005

Hawker Hunter F Mk 6/6A Mark 1 Guide
Michael Ovcacik
4+ Books, 2005

El 11 en la Mira de un Hawker Hunter – Las Operaciones y Blancoa Aereos de Septiembre de 1973
General Mario Lopez Tobar
Editorial Sudamericana, 1999

Hunters: The Hawker Hunter in British Military Service
Martin Bowman
Stroud, 2002

Hawker Hunter, Modern Combat Aircraft
Robert Jackson
Ian Allan, 1982

Best of the Hunter Breed: An Operational History of the Hawker Hunter FR.10
Nigel Walpole
Pen & Sword, 2006

Black Arrows, Blue Diamonds: Leading the Legendary RAF Flying Display Teams
Brian Mercer
Pen & Sword, 2006

Cold War, Hot Wings: Memoirs of a Cold War Fighter Pilot 1962-1994
Chris Bain
Pen & Sword, 2007

Hawker Hunter
Barry Jones
Crowood, 1998

Hunter: A personal View of the Ultimate Hawker Fighter
Roy Braybrook
Osprey, 1987

Hawker Hunter 1951-2007
David Griffin
Lulu Enterprises, 2007

Hawker Hunter
Tim McClelland
Crecy, 2008

Hawker Hunter: Fifty Golden Years
Raymond Deacon
Vogelsong, 2001

Test Pilot
Neville Duke
Wingate, 1953

Neville Duke's Book of Flying
Neville Duke
Cassell, 1954

Hawker Hunter Strsberedd!
Sune Blomqvis
Almqvist & Wiksell Tryckeri, Sweden, 1994

Hawker Hunter (Chile) FGA.71/FR.71/T.72 Serie Aeornaval 7
Claudio C. Godoy & Jorge N. Padin
Capital Federal, Argentina, 1994

Swiss Hunter
Peter Gunti & Peter Lewis
Sentinel Aerospace Ltd, 1994

Lengends of the Air 1 – Hawker Hunter Sabre/MiG-15
Stewart Wilson
Aerospace Publications, Australia, 1995

Hunter Fascination
Christophe Donnet
Schuck Verlag, Switzerland, 1995

Hunter – ein Jäger fur die Schweiz
Oliver Borgeaud
Autoren, Switzerland, 1997

RAF Hunters in Germany
Gunther Kipp & Roger Lindsay
Kipp/Lindsay, 2003

Index

Please note: this index does not reference appendices, walk-arounds or tables.

F.4 WV371/N, 74 Sqn. Note the nervous sideways glances at the mascot... *(© John Adams Collection)*

In tight with the Hunters of the Patrouille Suisse as they bank over the Swiss countryside *(© Swiss Armed Forces)*